The Horse I Belong To

The Horse
I Belong To

How a Misused, Almost Forgotten
Grade Mare Showed Me the Way

STEPHANIE ROGERS

Published by Horsetalker, LLC, Pawling, New York

ISBN: 978-0-9982516-0-8

Printed in the United States of America
Book design by Susan Hood
www.SusanHoodDesign.com

PHOTO CREDITS

Author: pp. 21, 26, 136, 139, and 247
Candace Maheu: p. 250
Kathy Matthews: p. 112
Allison McCauley: front and back covers, frontispiece, pp. 53, 55, and 97
Joseph Muskus: p. 137
Laura Ryan: pp. 161 and 162
A kind bystander took the photographs on pp. 248 and 249.

The author created the glossary illustrations on pp. 264, 265, and 267.

The author and Doris Tomaselli created the Horsetalker logo.

This book is dedicated to Mom and Dad.
You'd be so happy for me.

Dear Lauren,
There is no destination —
The journey is all.

Stephanie

Contents

Contents

Contents

Preface

This is primarily a story of healing; but, since it takes place in the domain of horsemanship, I am aware that many of my readers may be unfamiliar with terms common to that pursuit. As a result, I have included a glossary, which I hope will clarify terms that may be new to the general public.

Further, while it is the convention to refer to unnamed horses with the pronoun *it*, I bridle at using a pronoun equally applicable to inanimate objects to refer to these grand, majestic, and beautiful creatures who have given so much to humankind in general, and me, specifically. I am also keenly aware that, in a larger sense, the pronoun *it* dehumanizes, allowing us to care less about those we apply it to, human or not, and is a gateway to destructive thinking, cruelty, and abuse. So, in this book, I refuse that convention and refer to all creatures as "he" or "she."

—Stephanie Rogers
February 10, 2016

The Horse I Belong To

Introduction

Two damaged creatures, scarred inside and out by their early encounters with humans. Two damaged creatures, anxious, withdrawn, suspicious, but keeping one tiny part of their hearts secure, protected, in the frail hope that someday, they would meet the one they could let in. The one they could trust. The one who would understand them, love them, cherish them. Two damaged creatures against all odds encountered each other, and in each other found the one they needed, and these two damaged creatures after a lifetime of distress began to heal each other. One of them was an abandoned mare called Cheyenne. The other one was me.

Even in our relatively enlightened now, it is a human tendency to extract ourselves from the continuity of life on this planet, to the extent that we even refer to nonhumans as "animals," as if we weren't one ourselves. This way of thinking has allowed us to exploit them, consume them, and dismiss them as partners or teachers, because, of course, what can a mere "animal" have to teach that holiest of holy, us. Well, quite a lot, I discovered.

All animals, I suspect, but horses for sure, exist in a state of awareness that every wisdom tradition on Earth urges us to strive for—presence. The here and now. Undistracted by our commercialism and our toys, they see the world, hear it, smell it, participate in it with a fullness humans seek and only achieve with attentive pursuit. To live in the mind of a horse is to live in a healthy place. In an unperturbed state (meaning one in which humans have not abused or perverted them), horses live in the moment, hold no grudges, learn their lessons, and move on. Horses are honest. They do not feel sorry for themselves, fret over their appearance, worry about growing older. They simply cope. Leadership is earned, and while it may be challenged, it is respected. They are forgiving. This is the prescription for an enlightened life, no matter what your species is.

Their senses are so much more developed than ours, that an industry has arisen around using their hyper-awareness to help physicians and psychologists diagnose and treat mental, emotional, and behavioral imbalances among humans, because the horse immediately sees what it might take the human months to uncover. Anyone who rides is familiar with this—the horse knows as soon as he sees you how well you can ride, and treats you accordingly.

Horses are also effective in treating problems like cerebral palsy, ADHD, dementia, autism, and a range of other disorders that continues to expand—beyond the gifts of strength and mobility, the motion of the horse communicates to the equivalent muscles and nerves in the human, stimulating them even when the human cannot. Even more remarkable, however, is what a horse can do for the heart. It is a truism that "there is something about the outside of a horse that is good for the inside of a [hu]man" (Winston Churchill, brackets mine). I have seen for myself the transformation that occurs when a child is taken from a wheelchair, put on a horse, and a kid who couldn't walk instantly becomes bigger, stronger, and faster than anyone else.

And, of course, there is my own, personal transformation.

Both Chey and I had had difficult lives, not through any intent of those around us to hurt us, but merely through ignorance and misunderstanding. Chey handled it better than I did. She became balky and difficult. I became an addict, using a variety of substances and behaviors to suppress the pain of living long enough to keep on living, although at times it was close. Even when I made the decision to change my life in pursuit of something I had always dreamed of, the universe was not immediately forthcoming in granting me what I sought. In fact, even after I was trained by professionals, even after I had horses, I was so beaten down, injured, and disappointed, that by the time Chey came into my life, seven years ago as I write this, I was not certain I would ever ride again. As they say, you should see us now.

In changing my life from finance to horses, I made the first great discovery: It is always better to reach for something you love, than run from something you hate. My life with Chey led to a continuum of growth, fueled by a new worldview. I was introduced to the horse way of seeing things, quite different from the negative, defeatist, self-pitying gestalt in which I had lived my entire life. I discovered: the power of gratitude to lift you above the petty frustrations of the quotidian; the sense of peace you feel when you have trust in another; the rewards of having someone in your life to love and to care for; the excitement of growing in ability, in feeling, and in understanding something you did not before.

3

But the most important thing this horse did for me, which no one else had been able to do, was to make me think differently about *me*. That is how she changed my world. When you believe you are worthless, stupid, ugly, unlovable, you will live in a world that confirms those beliefs. I know this for a fact, because that is where I lived until she came into my life. When this horse began to trust me, respect me, when she started coming to me when she saw me even though she knew she was going to work, she began to make me feel differently about me. As I saw her efforts to meet more demanding requests—as I saw her responses change from fearful to purposeful—she rewrote the book of me. I felt valued, worthy, accepted—and when 1,000 pounds of breathing bone and muscle believe in you, it is powerful medicine. She took me out of that toxic world of criticism and judgment that always found me lacking, and brought me into a world of balance and motion, poetry and music, awareness, presence, softness, gratitude and, after a lifetime of not even believing in it, joy. This is our story, but not all of it. We have gone on to achieve remarkable things, and while the healing is not yet finished, this was its beginning. It did not happen for me with the psychologists, the therapists, the medication, or even with the other horses I'd known. It took this particular horse. This special horse, this ordinary, extraordinary horse. The horse I belong to, now and forever.

Mom

2005 was a very good year for very bad things. It was the year we became acquainted, briefly, with Terry Schiavo. It was the year we lost Pope John Paul II. It was the year Hurricane Katrina ate New Orleans. It was the year my mother died.

It was, mercifully, precipitous. She had a stroke on Thursday. She was alone for about twenty minutes before the neighbor Life Alert notified got into the house. I was at work in my office in midtown Manhattan when I got word she had been taken to Queens Hospital Center, and I headed there immediately. I stopped only to pick up a couple of sandwiches at a shop on Queens Boulevard. My mother loved a nice sandwich, and I hoped she'd be pleased. "Turkey tower and a tuna LT on whiskey down!" yelled the counterman, translating my order for a turkey club and a tuna sandwich with lettuce and tomato on rye toast.

When I got there, she was on a gurney in the emergency room. She was conscious, but barely, and was trying to speak but the consonants weren't there. She was weakly waving her hand. I told her it was OK, I was here now, and I wasn't going to leave. There were attendants with her, and a very serious but sympathetic doctor asked if he could speak with me. He informed me that she had had a massive stroke. He told me, slowly and carefully, that a surgical intervention was possible, but that it had about an 80 percent success rate, and that was based on a forty-year-old patient. If successful, it would require six months of recovery. He was kind enough to repeat everything he told me on the phone when I called my sister to tell her (she lived in the city, on the Upper West Side). He recommended, if we chose this option, moving her immediately to Long Island Jewish where they had a superior cranial surgery department. He also told me, quite pointedly, that I did not have a lot of time to make a decision. Minutes. Or it would be too late. They were shaving her head now, in case I decided for the surgery. Your head does funny things in a crisis. Mine figured I wouldn't be needing the sandwiches.

My heart stopped, and my mind spun. My mom was eighty-eight years old. The only thing she had ever wanted to be was a housewife, mother, and grandmother. In fact, she had difficulty imagining why any woman would want to be anything else, which was a source of contention between us for a long time. She lost my dad when she was fifty-four, my sister was twenty-one, and I was sixteen; she had no grandchildren. She was the youngest of five, and her brother and sisters were gone. Her friends from the old neighborhood were almost all gone. Over the last few years, she had been preparing for . . . this.

A few years ago, she got a financial adviser, and I found her a lawyer specializing in elder law. Over these years, she began transferring her assets to my sister and me so that we could avoid probate, since there is no "estate" if you already own the asset.

The last bit was to make us signatories on her bank accounts; we had just signed on the final account last week. She made a point of telling me that, when the time came, I shouldn't be too sad, because, frankly, she was ready.

My sister was for doing whatever it took. I was for letting her go. As most of us would, my mother prized her independence. She had a current DNR and had made it very clear to me that she did not want to linger. The last thing my mother would have wanted was to spend her last six months in a hospital bed, intubated, with my sister and me visiting once a week.

So I gave away the sandwiches, and we let her go. They put her on palliative care, which meant a morphine drip to ensure she was comfortable, but no ventilator, no feeding tube. She spent two more days in the hospital, in a coma. The last thing I said to her was, "You did a great job, Mom, and we love you." I think it got through.

In the Jewish calendar, 2005 was a leap year. The Jewish calendar follows a lunisolar cycle, similar to the Babylonian calendar, which is eleven days short of the sidereal year. To correct for this, there is an extra month inserted every six or seven years in a nineteen-year cycle. My mother died on II Adar II; the second day of the leap month of Adar. I was at home, in bed with my cat Goodwife Cozy sleeping next to me. Suddenly, in the middle of the night, Goody jumped up and meowed urgently, poking at me with her paw. I woke up and said, "What is it, Goody? What's the matter?" I had rarely seen her so disturbed. Then the phone rang. I stumbled out of bed to answer it. It was the hospital calling to tell me that Mom was gone. How about that? Goody already knew.

The loss of a parent is like the destruction of the world you know. They say losing a spouse or a child is more painful, but I had no spouse and no children. I was in shock for quite a while.

When I came out of it, I realized something with the greatest clarity I had ever experienced.

I had always dreamed of a life with horses. My first memory is of opening my eyes on my fourth birthday and seeing a rocking horse at the foot of my bed. I rode it vigorously in front of the television, as my mother ironed, watching westerns. I collected pictures and statues, I lingered over tack catalogs, I spent my babysitting money on an hour with a horse in every local park and vacant-lot riding stable in the five boroughs. I wore my red cowboy boots everywhere to my mother's consternation. When I grew up, every vacation was to go someplace where I could ride horses. How I loved horses. But to be realistic, I lived in New York City, I wasn't rich, and a life with horses was just not something a nice Jewish girl did, unless your father is Michael Bloomberg, of course. But I knew I'd get there someday. Much as I hated my job and was fraying under the pressure, I was well paid, I had health coverage, dental coverage, eye coverage, four weeks' paid vacation, lots of perks, and, well, you don't just leave that to jump off a cliff into an absurd child's fantasy. Plenty of time. Someday.

The personal cataclysm of my mother's death made it terrifically clear that, in fact, I didn't have forever. I was fifty-three. The number of "somedays" was not infinite. It was shocking. It was galvanizing. I started to think about making a Very Big Change.

What Came Next

By this point, I had been working in finance and I was a vice president in the mergers and acquisitions department of an international bank. LBOs—remember them? Leveraged[1] Buyouts. It was an area of finance as high-risk as rodeo. It was rock 'n' roll finance.

I was making good money but working sixty-, eighty- and sometimes hundred-hour weeks did not leave a lot of time for anything else. An example: One Good Friday, I had come into the office because I was working on a deal and was still there at 4:00 a.m. Saturday. Part of every credit proposal was a cash flow model, in which the income statement and balance sheet generated the cash flow statement. The numbers had to flow, so we

---

1. In finance-speak, "leverage" is another word for debt, since debt "leverages" up the returns on equity, as will be explained later. Leverage also ratchets up risk significantly—the more leverage, the more interest expense, which is a non-productive expense that eats up cash flow, and hence entails more risk of default or business failure.

could project into the future and see how much cash would be available to pay us back. Theoretically.

I was not good with numbers. I was struggling. After twenty straight hours on the computer, I still couldn't get the numbers to balance, and I kept repeating dead ends in the model I had already tried hours before. A couple of associates bombed into the analysts' bullpen, saw me, and blurted, "You! You got a passport?" Yes, I did have one. "Good, you're going to Helsinki. There's a car waiting for you. Get a change of clothes; your ticket is at the airport. When you get to Helsinki, deliver these deal books." They handed me a heavy document case.

"I . . . uh, I don't have any money." (That was the least of my concerns, but it's what came out.)

"Wait here!" They flew out of the bullpen.

A moment later, they were back with a large handful of cash. "Here's a thousand dollars. Go." This was 1988, by the way. A thousand dollars was something back then. So I went. I don't even remember what the deal was, but I remember I spent more time traveling to and from Helsinki than I spent in Helsinki. Helsinki is at sixty degrees north latitude (the Arctic Circle is at sixty-six degrees), and I do remember that the sun was still out at 10:00 p.m. on that Easter weekend in 1988. That was cool.

About that job: When I was a little girl, I would talk to my dad about The War, which was still recent history when I was born. We would watch the movies and I would ask him if it was really like that. And he would say that there was no way you could exaggerate the noise, the chaos, the stress. Now, I was not in a war zone, to be sure. But I can say that the pressure of being in the mergers and acquisitions group of a major money center investment bank in the 1980s and 1990s was astronomical. Hundred-hour weeks are not an exaggeration. You might be on five, six, seven deals at once, billions of dollars in transactions, millions of dollars in fees, deadlines everywhere; for filings, for commitments, for issuances and no excuses for not having anyone's transaction your absolute priority. Confidentiality was key, and minding your p's and q's was a full-time job, in addition to the six or seven other full-time jobs you had. It was only exhaustion, medication, tobacco, and alcohol that kept the anxiety from being fatal.

I really had no talent for numbers, as my superiors were well aware. Because of this, I slept even less than the typical analyst, who likely scored over 785 on the math SAT compared to my 520. And while I was intelligent and organized, it was always a close thing as to whether I would actually drown in the numbers, or not, as I struggled against time and anxiety to wrestle them into line. I kept my job because I was smart, I worked my brains out, and I wasn't afraid to appear stupid by asking the questions everybody had but didn't want to ask out loud. And I was an excellent communicator. My first attempt at a career had been in theater, so I knew how to act the part, project an intention. Since the Credit Committee might see thirty proposals/presentations a week, their gratitude for clarity was sufficient to compensate for my numerical immaturity. As a result, after a few years I was making six figures. At the very bottom of them, but six figures nonetheless. Not only did I have no time to spend anything; there was nothing I wanted but a horse, so those savings mounted up.

When my mother got a financial adviser to help her plan for "the future," I was in a position to understand his recommendations and I was very pleased at the program he had worked out for her. I asked if he would like to take me on as a client. He was happy to. By now, I had bought a house just over the Dutchess County line with my then boyfriend, and I went up there with Goody every weekend. I was leasing horses and had begun working with several for other people. In fact, twice, people had offered to give me the horses I had been working with, but I didn't think it was fair to own a horse if you could only spend two or three hours a week with her. Even those few hours were putting a strain on my relationship with my boyfriend and co-house-owner. I wanted more "horse" in my life, but didn't know how I could get there, although I was pretty sure I wasn't making the most of my financial resources.

Hence, Lance.

I did cash flow projections for a living, so I had already made a cash-flow model of my current life. There were those who loved working on Wall Street, but for me, the pressure was excruciating, the anxiety paralyzing. Some of my colleagues were very smart and had very big egos, and there were billions of dollars at stake. Many mornings, my anxiety was so great I couldn't get out of bed without calling my therapist and talking to him for an hour. I had to get out of that life but didn't know if I could. I was thinking of becoming a fitness instructor, a or masseuse . . . With that in mind, I kept track of every dollar I spent for a period of six months to see what my real cash needs were. Lance was delighted to hear this and asked for a copy.

We scheduled a meeting, and the first thing he said after the usual cordialities was, "Tell me your dreams. What do you want more than anything?" I didn't even have to think about it. "A life with horses." "OK," he said. "Let's take a look at that."

He approved of my asset allocation but had better information about how to maximize the returns from each asset class I had chosen. He diversified me into things I hadn't thought about, like REITs. He put the numbers together, projecting them at realistic growth rates based on all the data in the world. We had another meeting, and he said, "Well, Steph. You can do this."

Whoa. Wait a minute. You mean . . . now?

"Yes, you can do this."

It took my breath away. I couldn't believe it. What about emergencies, accidents, unexpected expenses? I'll never make any money again, if I leave this now. Health care? Dental?

"You can do this. You have an acceptable margin of safety, if you remain within the budget you've been living in for the last six months. I have your expenses growing with the twenty-year average inflation rate, and you can still do it. You can keep your house and your apartment, and still do it."

I needed to think about this. I was like an animal that has been in a cage for so long, that when you open the door, rather than dash to freedom, it shrinks in fear.

I couldn't do it. But then Mom died, and there was a modest inheritance, adding to my margin of safety as well as creating a sudden realization of my mortality. Still no . . . no. I can't. But . . . but . . . I also knew I couldn't live with the pressure of my job too much longer. I had been doing it almost twenty years. I hated it. It demanded more than everything I had, and it was just killing me.

And the job did kill people. We were all shocked when our colleague TD keeled over at his desk. He was a man in his forties, had a family. He had been talking to his daughter on the phone, probably apologizing for having to work late again, telling her he loved her. He had a heart attack and died with the phone in his hand. I could see that being me someday, if nothing changed.

I decided a prudent move would be to get a better sense of what a life with horses would actually be like. I had already discovered, during my life in the theater, that what you think a thing will be is not always the same as what it is.

I thought the theater, living in a world of ideas, getting to be someone else, would be wonderful. The accolades, the applause. The admiration of millions. It didn't work out that way. It was endless rejection, which became immobilizing for someone whose self-esteem was as low as mine. Coming three hours early to sign up for an audition, and being number 634 on the list.

When I joined Actors' Equity in 1975, I thought it would be better. But that just meant instead of competing against other wannabes like me, I was competing against people destined for greatness. My best shot was a callback for the role of Rizzo in the original *Grease*. I lost it to some girl . . . what was her name . . . oh, yeah, Adrienne Barbeau.

I loved the theater. But when I realized that the theater could live without me, I knew I had to find a way to live without the theater. That wasn't the only thing that could live without me, either. That same year, I'd married a guy with musical leanings whose career plan was to rely on me for the bills and his social connections for advancement. My marriage dissolved when he moved in with one of those connections, a woman who very thoughtfully paid for the divorce. That's when I decided if I couldn't have love, I'd go for money and went into finance. So, now, before I gave up an extremely lucrative employment, I decided to see if I couldn't get a little preview of this life I thought I wanted with horses without jumping off the bridge. I got an idea of how to do that.

For years, I had been subscribing to various horse magazines, my favorite being *Perfect Horse* by John Lyons. John is not the first to take a more humane approach to training horses, but he was a prominent name in the gentle ways of training horses. Think of the movie *The Horse Whisperer*, which was partly based on another of this sort of horseman, Buck Brannaman. Tom Dorrance is the modern granddaddy of the movement; Ray Hunt and many others are his disciples. What is now called natural horsemanship uses the same techniques an alpha mare uses to guide, correct, discipline, and reward the members of her herd. It does not use pain or fear to dominate the animal.

This is not new: Xenophon in about 400 B.C. broke from the practices of his time to urge a more humane approach to handling horses. Yet, sadly, for the last five thousand years, prevailing wisdom has permitted such practices, and devices, as would strain the definition of cruelty to the very edge of inconceivable. Thank heavens, things are changing now.

Anyway, John offered a training program for those seeking to advance along his path. His ranch is in Colorado, and you needed to bring two horses. That was a little far for me, and I didn't even have one horse. But there was a reputable trainer who had completed and "graduated" from John's extensive course whose facility was about an hour away from my upstate house. He and his partner offered a professional horse trainer certification program.

Sounded like what I was looking for. I even met the guy (we'll call him Carl) and his partner (we'll call her Terry) at a Nutrena expo in Stamford, Connecticut, and I really liked him. He talked about the important things to know when you're training horses and pointed out that every interaction with a horse is training them, for better or for worse, so it pays to know what you're doing. (Incidentally, that is also true for any interaction you have with another person. The overlap between successful relationships with horses and successful relationships with people was to prove absolutely astonishing.) At the end, he opened it up for questions. I had one: "How do you know when to stop cuing the horse?"

"That's a great question," he said. "Come on up here!"

I got up sheepishly and joined him on the stage. "Here," he said, handing me one end of a lariat and backing away so it was stretched taut. "You're the horse. Close your eyes. Do NOT let go."

I closed my eyes, and he started whanging that rope around so hard I jumped. He kept whanging. I hopped and twisted and when I took a step backward, *bam!* the rope immediately stilled. Oh. I get it. "Is it clear?" he asked. Yup. You stop asking when the horse does it. Horse training 101.

So I decided to take their course. It was expensive, but I was making good money, and I opted to go for it in lieu of my usual summer vacation in Wyoming. I have been riding horses since I was four, but I was getting too old to get badly hurt again. If nothing else, I would learn best practices, how to keep safe, and I always felt that being able to communicate with horses would be the highest calling I could ever aspire to. I had come to feel very close to John over the years of reading his gentle how-tos, and I felt very excited that this might really be the start of a dream.

The first module I took was called Beginning Under Saddle. It started at the end of July. I needed to bring a horse. As I said, I had been working with people's horses at some of the local barns on the weekends, and one lady allowed me to use her guy in the program. She had the horse trailer and everything. They hauled the horse out to Mooreville, New York, across the Hudson, with me leading the way in my Jeep. I got a room in a Super 8 nearby, apparently very popular with long-haul truckers. I could barely contain my excitement at the thought of the course, becoming a horse trainer, and best of all, spending all day with horses. This was gonna be great.

The Program

I woke up on the first day of the three-week program and gorged on the bagels, coffee, and reconstituted (orange?) juice offered courtesy of the Super 8. I even brought my own travel cup from Advanced Auto Parts—made me feel more cowboy. I got it at the bank meeting for the acquisition of Advanced Auto Parts, which took place in the Intercontinental on 50th Street between Fifth and Sixth Avenues on the morning of September 11, 2001. Yeah, that's where I was that day. But I wasn't thinking about that. It was 2006, and 9/11 was still pretty fresh, but I was completely focused on the beginning of a fifty-year dream.

I had equipped myself the way I would for Wyoming: riding boots, jeans, serious leather work gloves, big hat. Sunscreen. Water bottle. And then, for this program, notebook, pencil, and two pens in case one failed. I wasn't going to let a morsel of information get past me. After a last refill at the coffee station, I hopped in my Jeep and drove the fifteen minutes or so to Carl's facility. Like I was about to enter Candy Land.

The place was about twenty acres, roughly carved out of a hill. Carl's pleasant and airy house was on the "lobby" level. Then, the barn and office on the first sublevel, a round pen and a group of paddocks about even with it, a large riding ring on the second sublevel with more paddocks below. Most of the horses who lived here were in the upper paddocks; the horses of the people taking the program were in the lower. There were a few other horses down there, too, who were there to be trained or otherwise used in the program.

The coffee was gurgling in the tack room, and we all gathered in the office above the barn, where we were to go through some preliminaries, including of course introductions.

"Well, welcome!" beamed Carl, in a voice that could not have been better tuned for the purpose. He was a stocky man in his late fifties or early sixties, strong handed, heavy spurred, with the intricately wrought belt and buckle you expect on a cowboy. He was handsome. It was a little shocking when he took his cowboy hat off to reveal that he was bald. He introduced his partner, Terry, a tall slender woman with delicate features, red hair, and sparkly green eyes who looked like she was accustomed to being looked at, since she undoubtedly was, a lot. She wore breeches in the English style with paddock boots.

"Welcome to the program. We're going to be spending a lot of time together over the next three weeks, so why don't we start with each of you introducing yourselves and telling a little about your background with horses."

There were five of us in this program. A guy, who looked like a young Montgomery Clift, worked on a farm nearby where he breezed racehorses. (Breezing means taking young, lunatic thoroughbreds who have barely been broke to carry a rider and running them around a track at full gallop.) He brought a gorgeous dappled gray Arabian to the program. A girl of about eighteen with a truck, a trailer, and a high-class, well-trained reining mare, already looked as if she knew plenty about horses. A woman of about my age brought her two big, beautiful hunters to the program. She worked in the pharmaceutical industry. Another young woman, a big girl with a big smile and a big talent with horses, had a big, rambunctious thoroughbred. And . . . uh, me. Nothing but dreams and summer vacations, bringing my friend's horse, a young-ish black gelding who had been handled by people who meant well but didn't know what they were doing—resulting in a horse who knew how to get exactly what he wanted from them. He would throw a tantrum, balk, refuse, and they would back away.

But it was all right. Despite the fact that everyone else there had been handling horses for years and had their own, or several of their own, there was no suggestion that I was out of my depth. On the contrary: I was to find out that just because someone has owned horses for years does not mean they are handling them effectively. I was in just the right place. As I was to feel many times over the coming months and years, I just wish I could have done it sooner.

Carl and Terry were a perfect pair. He had been a senior executive in a resource company, but had been working with horses all his life. She was a certified Centered Riding instructor, a tai chi instructor, and had a master's in education. He took the lead on handling the horses; she took the lead on equitation and designing the program. It was a wonder to see the respect they offered each other, even while they might argue on when we should do something or why it was important. One assumed they were married, and they were, but not to each other. They were a terrific team.

"OK," Carl said. "We're going to go over a few things up here. Then you'll get your horses and we'll meet in the ring and get to work. I assume all your horses are halter broke and can be saddled, bridled, and mounted. That is the starting point for this program."

He and Terry then took turns talking about basic principles, first of which is safety. The three rules of horsemanship they, along with a great many other professionals, recognize as foundational:

1. You can't get hurt.
2. The horse can't get hurt.
3. The horse has to be calmer after the lesson than it was before.

Rule number one would be very important to me. I was used to pushing myself beyond all limits, I had a drive to please, and I was determined to be the best there ever was. But here, it was time to get serious. My exposure to horses so far had been to the poor animals in the riding stables who get pounded by six or seven riders of uneven ability every day; or working cow horses who routinely cover twenty to thirty miles six or seven days a week over rough country with two hundred pounds of saddle, rider, water, slicker, and lunch on their backs. I was about to enter the real world. Real horses, like real life when you get back from that vacation, can be very, very different and not nearly as cooperative or forgiving.

In this program, we would be working on the ground and on board a bunch of horses with various levels of training, all together in a ring that seems big until you see how fast a panicky horse can cross it. We were reminded to stay alert, to use our peripheral vision at all times when horses were in the ring. When a thousand pounds of frightened muscle starts to accelerate, you don't want to be in the way.

20

Then we went to get our horses.

It turned out the one I brought was unsuitable for this program. Although I had been riding the gelding at home, here, he was a nut job, refusing to stand for saddling, refusing to be tied, and once in the ring, he tore the lead line out of my hands and galloped away. Carl calmly caught him and returned him to me. "This may not be the right program for this horse. Level One would be perfect for him. Put him away and take out that sorrel gelding with the blaze down there with the mare. You can use him. His name is Poker Joe."

Poker Joe saw me coming and looked worried. He was one sorry-looking horse. Not abused or anything; just obviously low man on the totem pole. He was all scarred up by more dominant horses, and he was skinny—clearly, the last one to get to the food, if there was any left. His mane and tail were straggly with neglect and uncertain nutrition. But he had big wistful

My first sight of Poker Joe

21

STEPHANIE ROGERS

eyes, and a snaggle lip, and he came along willingly enough, as if he thought that this time, things might be different.

I saddled him up and joined the others in the ring where Carl had started day one of the three-week program.

We worked eight to ten hours a day, in the dusty arena, in the sun, in the heat, in the saddle with our water bottles perched strategically on the fence so we could reach them without having to dismount. We rode our own and other horses. We learned the grammar of pressure and release with which we built an ever-increasing vocabulary. Horses, of course, do not speak as we do. They express themselves through posture and movement, and Carl and Terry introduced me to the language that enabled me to request and receive increasingly complex and demanding movements. I thought I had died and gone to heaven.

It was not easy. We are analytical animals; horses are not. For so much of humankind's relationship with horses, we just expected them to understand us and if they didn't turned to pain or fear to compel them to our will. But I was learning the horse way of communicating, and I ate it up. Pressure and release. As little as possible, but as much as necessary. Step one for this program: a little pressure on the rein to get a "give," the slightest movement of the horse's jaw in the direction of the pull. No punishment, just reward for the right answer. In fact, reward the try, even if you don't get the answer you are seeking. How that concept became important to me in my human relationships. It's quite remarkable what happens when instead of cranking on people for failing, you start rewarding even the try. The same thing happens with people as with horses; you get more try. And in Carl's words: "First you get it, then you get it consistently, then you get it pretty."

Hour by hour, we used too much, we used too little, what worked on this horse didn't work on that horse, we tweaked it

22

here and cheated it there, but eventually, we conditioned them, taught them, and they us, that giving to pressure is the easiest way to release the pressure, and we got our "give." From getting barely any response when we first tugged the rein, after a bit the horses would touch their noses on the stirrup and all we had to do was pick up the rein. They had learned what it meant and eventually moved when they saw us lift our hand, without even feeling any pressure. We had trained them. It was amazing.

Why would we want a horse to move its nose to the stirrup? Because no human can control a horse. It is too big, too strong. Our only hope is to control one little piece of them. And if, for example, the jaw, or the shoulder point, or the withers, or the hindquarters stop moving, pretty soon the whole horse stops moving. The converse is also true. You can't make a horse move, but if you can make the tip of its right ear move forward, pretty soon the rest of the horse will be moving forward, also.

What we were really doing was learning to communicate in horse, but this principle of pressure and release is really universal. For them, the reward is the release. It's as simple as that. In this program, it was made clear that the reward is not food[2] or hugs and kisses. Well, maybe hugs and kisses the first time the horse gets it, but not after that. After that first good response, you have a right to expect certain things. It's about leadership. It made me realize: You need to be careful about what behavior you reward—both with horses and with people. Think of how many times you've seen parents hush a noisy kid at the mall with an ice cream cone. It trains the kid how to get an ice cream cone, and later, anything else he or she wants. Working with horses makes you start paying attention to this kind of thing. In

2. The way I was taught, food is a bribe; it is not training and it is not leadership.

the coming years, a lot of things would change in the way I treated people and let them treat me, because of what I learned from horses.

Then I started discovering other marvelous things. The quality of movement was different depending upon how you asked. If you asked for a turn by turning the horse's nose, you got it, but it was a gangly swinging affair. If you asked for it from the withers, it got better. If you asked from the shoulders, it was smoother still. Movement that originates from the core is more balanced and pleasant that movement that originates from an extremity. I remembered the ballet lessons I had as a little girl, and a window opened for me as I thought about equine disciplines from reining to dressage with greater comprehension. This was learning that literally took me to a new world.

We explored movement I hadn't known horses were capable of: lateral movement, leg yields, a lovely diagonal movement the horse makes while holding his body straight that looks like the two of you are bouncing along in a big bubble. Side passes. Collection. Extension. Working walk. Oh my goodness, I was in a candy store.

At the end of the day, we would take care of the horses we'd been riding and head back to our respective motels and inns. I grabbed Chinese or Italian and dove into my notebook at the Motel 6 as the sound of big rigs pulled into the parking lot under my window. I wrote frantically, trying to get it all down. Diagrams. Dotted lines. Arrows. Question to raise tomorrow. This was everything I'd hoped it would be. I was no longer reading about horses as I had been forced to do all my life. I was hands-on, dust in the teeth, sweat in the eyes, ache in the thighs working with horses all day long. I was too excited to sleep.

Day after day, we learned and then practiced increasingly demanding maneuvers. Terry schooled us in equitation, since it makes perfect sense that a poor rider will have only mild success in horse training, and I had some of the first riding lessons I'd ever had in my life. (I had had my first riding lesson in Paris a few years earlier, a jumping lesson, after my friend Christiane and I returned from riding a couple of magnificent Arabian stallions across Morocco for ten days. In the Paris lesson, we were jumping *sans étriers* [without stirrups], in a ring about the size of my living room. I went off and had an interesting interaction with a French chiropractor, but that is a story for a different day.)

I was coming to admire scraggly old Poker Joe. He was a sweet horse, if not the most handsome in his current state, and he patiently continued through the long, hot days in the saddle as I tried every wrong way to get what we were trying to get before I found a right way. He remained unfailingly attentive. And while he probably would have been justified in freezing up on me and saying *What the hell you want, lady?* he didn't. As we worked our way through the modules, I got softer in my hands and seat; he got smoother and lighter. I would look forward to seeing, grooming, and riding any horse, but I was getting to where there was a smile in my heart for Poker Joe. Horses are professionals at seeing into your heart, and he could tell where the warm spot was growing in me. It got to where when he saw me coming down the hill with the halter, he would move toward the gate to meet me.

Poor horse—he was about eight years old, and this must have been about the first time anyone treated him gently, groomed him with love, and really made an effort to "talk" to him. I heard he was bought off a hack line. From his earliest days, all he knew was strangers with limited abilities, pounding on his back, hauling on his mouth, banging on his sides, and beating him. Not everyone who rides hack horses is an ignorant wannabe cowboy, but when I look back on my own early days, riding

Not so worried anymore

those rent-a-horses through vacant lots in Queens, I continue to marvel that people don't get hurt more often than they do. It's a marvel the horses don't turn mean. Well, I guess some of them do and become dog food, but Poker Joe just endured. Maybe he wasn't too smart, and that's why he didn't explode. Maybe he was just kind.

We went through further modules, with a riding lesson included at some point every day. We went through troubleshooting: What do you do if the horse won't leave the gate? How do you get the correct lead? What if she won't stand still at the mounting block? This last proved quite interesting. There was an enormous Belgian in the program who topped out at more than eighteen hands. (A "hand" is four inches and it is measured from the highest thoracic vertebra, or the withers, which is where the neck and body meet.) That meant the horse we started calling Thor measured about six feet tall before you even got to his head and neck. A special mounting block had been constructed for him, with a platform about three feet off the ground so that you'd have a chance of getting on him. But he wouldn't stand by the mounting block.

Carl did his magic on him. He made Thor run around the ring except for when he was by the mounting block. There he could rest. Thor was not stupid. In no time at all, he realized the mounting block was the place you didn't have to work, and he was happy to stand there. A couple of the guys then picked up the mounting block to move it . . . and Thor followed it! Standing by the mounting block was never a problem for Thor again.

It was coming to the end of this three-week module, and I felt like I was eleven years old at horse camp, and the summer was coming to a close. I am not a morning person, but I had bounced out of bed and to the coffee machine, and then jumped into boots and jeans to race to the facility. To have a horse to catch and groom, to saddle up and know you'd spend the day learning what you'd always dreamed of learning about horses—I had in fact never been this happy, since those summer days at Rawhide Ranch. There were tests at the end of the program, one written and one practical. I got high marks on the written test. Like, 100 percent. The practical was: We had to ride a horse we had not yet ridden and evaluate him: Was he stronger to one side than the other? Would he pick up his leads? Did he have a good stop? et cetera. Carl and Terry, who knew the horse, would determine if we accurately evaluated him. Then, they would give us an assignment for that particular horse based on what we told them about him. For example, if the horse was gate sour, we had to cure him of that, get a good collected trot, and teach him to lie down with you in the saddle.

27

No problem!

I did very well, and I graduated, but my equitation was not quite good enough at that time for them to offer me their certification. At first, I was very disappointed in myself, but, on reflection, I realized what a treasure of an education I had received. What we win too easily, we value too lightly, as Thomas Paine says in *Common Sense*, and if horsemanship were easy, everyone would be able to do it. I came to understand that this course was not a destination, but an introduction to the journey; and that I would be on that journey for the rest of my life. "We're always beginners," another trainer said to me years later, and I realized that that is a much more productive way of looking at horsemanship, and, well, everything.

I had also recognized the pinprick of light behind a radical idea that had begun to enter my mind. Not since camp had I ridden the same horse so long and so regularly. Poker Joe wasn't going to win any prizes in anything, but he was a good, honest horse. I felt the warmest glow when I was near him and saw his recognition. This battered, young horse seemed astonished to be treated with affection and was at first hesitant in his responses to me as I groomed and stroked him while waiting for class to begin. I mean, he gave when I tugged on his rein, but in the downtime, he seemed amazed I was stroking him. He would turn his big scraggle-lip face and look at me, and say, *Gee, that's nice. What is that?*

I found out that the people who had bought him off the hack line had some intellectual limitations. So even after he had escaped the hack line, he was with people who were first of all unskilled with horses, which he was used to; but, second of all, couldn't recognize when he was trying to do what he thought they wanted. They had brought him to Carl's for training. My feelings for the horse soared. What a good soul, what a decent horse. He would be a good horse for me.

What???!!! What did you say??

Yes. He could be mine. This could be my first horse. I mean, I felt good about him. Good enough to have him. Confident enough about him to buy him.

Oh my goodness. I couldn't believe it. I couldn't believe the very thought. I have waited my whole life to have a horse, and here I was, in a time and a place where it could happen. I think I came close to fainting from excitement. It made sense. He was not expensive. I could keep him at the barn where I was already riding other horses. I had spent three weeks riding him, grooming him, working with him on the ground and in the saddle, training him. He was unfailing polite, gentle, willing. I knew this horse. I liked him. He liked me. Maybe the day had come. . . .

I couldn't make this decision alone. I called Jeff, dear friend and perpetual supporter, whom I knew from my earliest days in finance. Jeff has been there for me for every crisis of my life, in finance (there were many) and outside of it. I told him the story. Should I do it?

"Well," he said, "you've wanted this for a long time. I know you've always dreamed of having your own horse. You have all the pieces in place, what with your house upstate and the barn where you've been riding. Financially, it won't be a material burden. You know the horse, and you're among professionals who are in a position to guide you. I think the time and place are right."

Oh my goodness! Jeff, who is very, very smart and a very, very good friend, thought it made sense.

Then I called Bernie, dear Bernie, a companion from the trails of Wyoming. To know Bernie is to love Bernie. He was a businessman, CEO of his own company, retired. He took up riding horses in his sixties, and is a happy, optimistic, and just all around wonderful kind of guy as ever there is. "Well," he said, "I think you've gone about as far as you can as an amateur. If you want to do the things you've always talked about doing, I think the time has come to have your own horse."

Well, there you had it. Two of the three people whose opinion I valued most said, "Go for it." Number three would be Fred. I don't know why I didn't call Fred. He is a mathematics professor and it was summertime. Perhaps I didn't think I could reach him. But I think I know what he would have said: I had always dreamed of having my own horse. I had taken every step to educate myself. I was at a professional's facility, and the circumstances appeared optimal. So . . .

I talked to Carl about it. He thought it made sense and guided me in how to approach the owners. He gave me a template purchase agreement to be filled out with the details of the transaction. I didn't know anything about buying horses, but I did know that before you bought a horse, you should have a veterinarian thoroughly check him out. I said, "I guess I ought to get a vet check." "He's been here for months," said Carl. "You don't need a vet check."

I made an offer, the people wanted more, I offered a little more than I had at first and a little less than they asked . . . then they told me they had another horse and asked if I would like to look at that one. Actually, I didn't, but I was getting into the swing, and I went to their house where they had other horses hanging out in a bedraggled barbed-wired field. They got out the mare they had in mind. She stood nicely enough for saddling and she rode nicely enough and didn't rear, buck, spin, bolt, or kick. But she wasn't like Poker Joe. When I looked in her eyes, there was no "there" there. She did what she asked, but she kept herself apart—a condition I was to see in a lot of horses as the years passed. So no thanks. It was Poker Joe or nothing.

They relented and agreed to sell him to me. You'd laugh: He cost less than an average New York City month's rent. We agreed I'd pay half now and half when I came back for the next three-week session in a month. We signed the bill of sale Carl had printed out for us . . . and I had bought my first horse! A couple of the other students were there for the event, and Lynda, a friend from the program, took a picture of us: me and Poker Joe at the exact moment I became a horse owner for the very first time. To me, he was the most beautiful horse in the world, and he was mine. The dream of a lifetime, breathing softly right next to me.

"I have a horse!" I cried, delirious. I danced a little, Poker Joe watching curiously. Lynda was an old hand at this. "Oh, it'll be no time at all before you're saying 'my new horse' or 'my other horse.'" Maybe, but this was an extraordinary moment, and I could think of absolutely nothing else I wanted in the world. I had a horse. A beautiful horse. My own horse. I was so happy, I couldn't believe it was real.

To me, he was even more beautiful than Trigger.

Life with Horses Begins

I half-paid for my new horse and returned to work at the bank next Monday. I came back changed. I knew something I hadn't known before. I walked into my boss's office early and asked if it was a convenient time to talk to him.

Gavin, my boss, was a wonderful, intelligent, and talented man, and I had been instrumental in getting him hired, recommending him highly to my boss who was French and wanted an American's perspective on him. He was so gentle and thoughtful one wondered how he would fare in this snake pit. Despite those qualities, since he was enormously better suited to the work than I could ever hope to be, he had advanced quickly and was now my boss.

"Sure," he said. "How was your program?"

"It was great! It was just great and I bought a horse! Isn't he beautiful?" I blurted, and showed him the pictures. He smiled like the parent he was and looked at my very ordinary horse with sufficient generosity to agree. Then I steeled myself for what I wanted to say next. When he looked up from the picture to me, I said, "You know . . . I absolutely loved it. I've never loved doing anything as much as I loved spending eight to ten hours a day getting hot, dusty, and exhausted working with horses. And . . . you know . . . I have to believe . . . that if you ever find anything in your life that you love as much as I love horses . . . it is almost a sin against nature to deny it. So"—I took a deep breath—"I am informing you of my intention to resign." Oh my God, did I just say that? Did I really do it?

After an appropriate pause, Gavin sat back and smiled. "I can't say that it comes as a surprise, but I can say that we'll miss you. And congratulations on taking the jump to do something you really want."

Deep breath. We decided that August 28, 2006 would be my last day. It was time to make the rounds and tell my friends.

I went over to Chuck's desk. "Oh, hi, Steph! Hey, could I get those comps you did for R. H. Donnelly, I'm looking at Yellow Book and we need to turn this around by Wednesday, Ola needs . . ." "Whoa," I said. "I have news for you. I just resigned." "No! Really? Where're you going, Soc Gen? Hedge fund?"

These were reasonable questions under the circumstances. My answer was not. "Nope. I'm going to be a cowboy."

"Ha, you're kidding, right?" No. I wasn't. I had just quit my job as a vice president in the mergers and acquisitions group of an international financial institution to, among other things, shovel horse manure.

The word sped around the institution and was met with wonder by some, dismissal by others who were so into the game, all else faded beside the power of the next deal. A month passed while I shifted responsibilities and trained my replacement.

Then, on my last day, the department head threw me a big time party at La Mode, across the street on 53rd between Sixth and Seventh Avenues. My friends were happy for me, the juniors were happy for the free drinks, and with no little trepidation, I began my new life. With my new horse. My horse. Poker Joe.

A Hitch

Poker Joe stayed at Carl's for the few weeks between the beginning under saddle and advanced under saddle modules. It was still a dream come true. We were given homework in the beginning under saddle module, things our horses needed to be able to do to advance to the next level. I came out on weekends to ride Poker Joe and work toward those goals. I had expected my boyfriend of some fifteen years, J, who bought the house with me, to be happy for me; he most definitely was not. I just couldn't understand it. This was the first time in all the years we had been together that I had struck out for something on my own, and he was not pleased. I hated the job. It was killing me. I was getting drunk every weekend and sometimes, in between. I was desperate. What was this?

I was confused. Ten years prior to this, when he had suggested going in on the house with me, I thought that meant something. It did, but what it meant to him was very different from what it meant for me. To him, it was a business transaction. An investment. When I talked to him about my plans to quit banking and make a life with horses, he asked, "So you'll be living up there full-time?" "Yes!" I replied happily. "Well," he said, "maybe you ought to start paying me rent."

I was speechless. We owned the house fifty-fifty. I was so shocked at that response that I was unable to speak. Had I been a more complete person, I would have done more than just cried. But I wasn't, and I didn't. He insisted. Some remnant of self-respect piped up, and I told him that I'd talk to his two sisters about it, and if either of them thought it was fair, I'd do it. That ended the conversation, but not the friction that was to become more uncomfortable over time.

For most of my life, I have not been a good judge of people, or anything else, really. I wasn't wearing rose-colored glasses, exactly. It was more like not knowing what to think. I lived pretty much in my own head, because I was depressed, anxious, and afraid all the time. More on that later. But back to the program.

The Program Resumes

The arrangement with Poker Joe's owners was, that when I returned for the next module, I was to pay them the balance of what I owed on Poker Joe. I did; and for two thousand dollars, I had bought myself a real live horse. He was mine. I don't know how he felt about it, but I was beside myself with happiness and love. Poker Joe looked at me with big, quiet eyes, and it seemed to me that his scars were healing and his ribs a little less prominent.

On a September Monday in 2006, we assembled for the Advanced Under Saddle module. Most of us knew each other from before. A brief introduction in the office, and then we saddled our horses and met down in the arena.

We were happy and relaxed, veterans of the first three weeks, confident in our new skills and looking forward to what we would learn in the coming module. Right now, Carl was mounted, Terry was on foot, and Carl was talking about what we were about to work on; we were going to introduce lateral work, then move on to work on the cavaletti, jumping, collection, lead changes, rollbacks, and spins, a candy store of horsemanship to me. By the end of this module, we would be riding our horses without bridles, with nothing but a rope around their necks. Having already achieved apparent miracles in the first module, we already knew that all these incredible achievements were within our grasp, and we would be executing them, on multiple horses, in no time. The first time we sat here listening, we were anxious and scared. This time, we were confident and quietly excited. We knew we could do it. We had in the last program. This was going to be really cool. I was learning how to train horses, and for the first time in my life, it seemed like I was succeeding at something.

We prepared to work on the leg yield, and in a flash, the day turned ugly. I picked up Poker Joe's reins, and in an indefinable instant, he squealed and violently reared up, and up. I dropped the reins and grabbed his neck, but he kept going up, so high I knew I had to dive off. I feared he would go over backward, crushing me if I were still on board. I saw a circle of horrified eyes as I leaped off to the left, hitting the dirt, landing almost under the feet of two other horses, tucking and rolling hard. Monty Clift and the young woman had been mounted next to me, and later said they thought the horse was going to crash down on top of them, too. It was too fast for anyone to react.

OMG!

I shot up to my feet as quickly as I could, because the ground is a very bad place to be when you are among six or seven horses, one of whom is going crazy. Carl caught him, and of course, what I had to do was to get back on. You can't let a horse think that all he has to do is misbehave and he gets the day off. So Carl worked with Poker Joe a little, then held him while I got on, and we walked around a bit. I was barely moving, I was so scared, and it felt like my stomach was wrapped around my spine. Carl let go, and Poker Joe and I moved a few steps gingerly. Then Carl gave me a choice. I could continue to work with Poker, but if it happened again, we would have to work through it again; or, I could take another horse. I opted to take another horse. My heart rate was still over 150.

I put Poker Joe back in his field, and Carl looked carefully at his tack. He found a little tiny little bit of something sticky on the bit, but hesitated to say that was what had caused the eruption. Maybe it was a tick. Maybe Joe had Lyme disease. He suggested we get a blood test. And now, of course, after the last money had changed hands and there was no going back, that was what we did.

Meanwhile, I got Teak out of another paddock, a lovely bay Arabian, which is of course redundant, since every Arabian is fairy-tale beautiful. He was quiet and not hard to catch, so I saddled him up and joined the others in the arena. Life went on. My heart was with Poker Joe in his paddock, but Carl seemed to think this was probably nothing too extreme, and I rested on his vastly superior knowledge. I certainly hoped it wasn't. I mean, I finally get a horse, and after riding him for five weeks, he goes and explodes on me like that and . . . well, better not to think about it.

So, I rode Teak into the ring, and we started working on lead changes, cantering a circle right, trotting up the middle, and then cantering a circle left. Carl had placed cones in the middle of the arena to indicate where we were to trot. At first, four strides at the trot; then three; then two; the horses have the pattern now; then one, then, no trot at all, but a flying lead change in the waist of the figure eight! There was not a single horse who didn't finish the morning by delivering a perfect flying lead change in both directions. We put them up and went to lunch.

39

We finished the day with some equitation, and then went up to the barn to talk about saddles, saddle fit, and pads. Carl introduced us to a new space-age material pad, a closed cell thing that was amazing. It would shift to compensate for minor saddle fit issues and was better at transferring heat away from the horse's back than wool or felt. We took copious notes. By now, we students were bonding. That night, we brought a pizza back to the Motel Six and talked about the day, the program, and what we thought might be on the test.

When I went to sleep, I had The Dream. Since I've been small, I've had a recurring dream. I used to have it frequently, but I hadn't had it in a while. I am in a lovely wooded glen, on a lovely spring day, sunlight dappling down on the ground. There is a beautiful horse, just there, looking at me, saddled and bridled. I approach; she doesn't move. I reach for her; the horse nuzzles my hand. We spend a few moments like that . . . quiet . . . I'm stroking the horse. I pick up the reins to mount. I lift my foot, but just before I feel the weight of my foot in the stirrup, I wake up. I never get to ride. It was a painfully frustrating dream, but I had had it so often, I had gotten used to it.

The next day, bright and early, I drove singing to the facility and went out with a halter to catch Teak. He was different today. I wasn't sure if I was reading that correctly. I caught him anyway and started to groom him and tack him up. At one point, he swiped his head around and tried to nip me. *Whoa.*

When Carl and Terry showed up, I told them that Teak had tried to nip me when I cinched him up. Terry said, "Oh, just smack him. He does that."

Well, if you say so, but he was so different yesterday, and despite Terry's nonchalance, I was a little worried about him. I thought maybe he was sore from the saddle they had told me to use, so I got the super-duper space age pad and used that instead of the old wool one they had given me the day before. I cinched him up as gently as I could. He was not happy.

We were starting to assemble in the arena. I had a bad feeling about Teak. We were all mounted in a semicircle around Carl, who was talking about what we would do today. Then, I felt something very urgent, I don't know what it was, but I felt it from the horse and I shot my hand up and said, "Carl, I'm sorry to interrupt, and maybe this is partly because of yesterday, but I have a bad feeling about this horse, and I don't want to ride him."

"Let me get on that horse!" he grumbled. I jumped off, shaking, and Carl got on and he started loping Teak around the arena. Teak loped a circuit, and then, in perfect rhythm, he shoved his head between his knees and threw his hindquarters about ten feet into the air. He started bucking like a rodeo professional, massive, slow motion jackknives in the air. Carl looked shocked. He also looked terrified. Teak was dead serious about getting that man off his back and put his substantial muscle into it, as we stood around paralyzed on our horses and watched the wreck in progress. Teak grunted and gave one explosive buck, and Carl was launched over the six-foot fence, heading directly for the boulders that lined the hill beyond it. He grabbed the fence as he passed it upside down, and saved his life by slamming into it instead of the boulders. Terry screamed, "Catch the horse!" and ran for Carl. Monty leaned over to me. "Guess you were right," he mumbled.

Carl couldn't breathe. Terry raced him to the hospital. Cracked sternum, couple of ribs. The bruises were starting; we found out that half his body turned purple, and he wouldn't be able to ride for the next four months. *That could have been me,* I thought. Lynda, reading my mind, said, "You probably would have been killed." Uh, yeah.

When Terry came back that afternoon, we resumed. She told me to get another horse, Macadam, a gnarly-looking Appaloosa. I got him, tacked him up, and, legs shaking, heart thrumming, I got on weakly. *What was this one gonna do?*

However, the rest of the program proceeded uneventfully. I again got perfect marks on the written portion, but failed to get a "certifiable" grade in the practical exam. It turned out that Poker did indeed have Lyme disease, as did Teak, and as did every other horse in the paddocks on the east side of Carl's facility. The program was over for now. I aimed to take one more module the next summer, for which I had already paid. It was time to take Poker Joe home.

Poker Joe Comes Home

I had already arranged with Debbie that I would take a space at Ridgehollow. I was confident in Carl's confidence and learned that horses with Lyme disease respond well to treatment. A little doxycycline and Poker would be as good as new, and I would have my wonderful, well-trained, affectionate horse to play with and do shows with and everything.

I had spent a lot of time at Ridgehollow, riding a horse for the former owner, and Debbie and everyone else knew about the program I was taking. They knew I'd quit my job and wanted to be a horse trainer. "Maybe I can hang a shingle and train horses out here!" I chirped. And Debbie, being as good a person as she was, did not act in the least bit skeptical that I would be ready to make a living training horses after a nine-week course.

I didn't have a truck, or a horse trailer, and Deb recommended a fine Irish hostler who would trailer my horse for me; "I've a great open trailer," said he, "even a horz who won't go inna trailer for other people is happy tah go wit me." There is something about an Irishman that warms one, and I was proud and happy to load My Horse into his big open trailer and head back to his new home in Brewster.

Debbie was waiting for me smiling. "So, let's see your horse!" Poker Joe backed out nicely and stood calmly, his well-groomed chestnut coat glowing, his pale mane and tail beginning to fill out by now. I began to prate about all the things we'd done in the program, and how sweet and willing he had been, and how much I loved him. A few other boarders had gathered around, probably chuckling a little in their hearts about how finally having my own horse had turned me overnight into a ten-year-old girl with her first pony.

"Ya gonna ride him?" asked Lindsay. Lindsay is a heavy woman in her early fifties who liked to talk about her brilliant Grand Prix career (not), and is among the first to tell you how you should be handling your horse. She herself was almost never on her horse and always had an excuse for why. However, she did bathe him so much that one year, his legs got moldy.

"Of course!" I said. I broke out my brand-new gear, saddled him up, and grinning ear to ear, went into the ring.

The gang was there to watch. I was proud as a parent, and we walked and trotted and leg-yielded and side-passed over rails, the sun glinting off his well-brushed coat. When I touched him into a canter, we flowed across the ring in the most delightful rhythm until, without missing a beat, he bucked me off like a champagne cork popping.

"Oh!" I heard from five voices simultaneously. Debbie ran in to help me; someone else caught the horse. "I'm awright, I'm awright," I said, catching my breath. That was quite a bump. No matter how big the horse is, it's always a long way down.

"Maybe the doxycyline hasn't kicked in yet," Debbie said gently.

Debbie is one of the best people I've ever met. She had been a mounted police officer in New York City until a catastrophic accident split her skull in three pieces and ended her career with the force. It wasn't the horse's fault, she remembers that much—and the discharge of a firearm was involved, and Debbie has never been able to remember anything more about it. She was retired with a small disability pension, and now, she was managing this boarding facility. I have never heard her make a statement that wasn't kind, constructive, and true. I didn't know her before—perhaps it was the accident that made her incapable of falsehood or manipulation, but I suspect not. She is a hardworking, kind, generous, thoughtful, infinitely decent person. She must have been a terrific cop. I am very lucky I started my horse life with her in the picture.

"Let's take him to his paddock and let him chill out a little," she suggested. I tried to get my legs under me to get up. "No, no, no, it's OK. I'll unsaddle him and take him down. Your paddock is the corner one by the pond. You go over there and sit for a while. Drink some water. Have a cigarette." "Thanks," I sighed and, with Meryl's and Katy's help, I stumbled over to sit down on one of the chairs set up for us in the shade.

"Hmmph" I heard Lindsey huff. "Figures."

I came every day to groom my treasure, and every day, I saddled and bridled him and got bucked off. After about a month of this, Debbie said, "Maybe it would be a good idea to call someone," meaning a vet. We didn't think it was a training issue: I had just spent six weeks working with this animal; he was beautifully trained. Obviously, something hurt. At that time, a veterinarian much in favor at the barn was Dr. Amery, an equine chiropractor who had done wonders with several of the other horses. In the United States, in order to be an equine chiropractor, you must first be a board-certified veterinarian.

Dr. Amery, at that time, was in practice with Dr. Allen Schoen, a veterinarian who was instrumental in integrating Eastern and holistic healing practices, like acupuncture, into his equine practice. He is the author of *Kindred Spirits: How the Remarkable Bond between Humans and Animals Can Change the Way We Live*, and *Love, Miracles, and Animal Healing*.

So, we called Dr. Amery, who looks just like what you'd like a man who will treat your beloved horse to look like. He was a bit over medium height, lean, with attentive eyes and handsome features. He brought his veterinary and his chiropractic equipment with him. We brought up Poker Joe, who came willingly enough, and Dr. Amery looked him up and down and sideways, walking around him. He asked to see him walk and trot, up and down the driveway. We lunged him. He checked his teeth, palpated his legs, his back, his neck and head.

"OK," he said. "Let me try something."

He got up on his chiropractic block (a secure thing to stand on so he could manipulate a horse's back) and started working. Dr. Amery exuded kindness and warmth, and Poker Joe trusted him almost immediately. Performing chiropractic care on a horse takes a lot of *oomph*, but Poker Joe seemed OK with it. Dr. Amery finished up by getting off his block, standing directly behind the horse, grabbing his tail up high with both hands, and pulling back with a jerk I thought would get him kicked into Connecticut, but we just heard a *POP!* and Poker Joe gave a deep sigh.

"There is tenderness in T13, 14, and 15, a mild subluxation, and the supporting muscles have gotten strained trying to protect it. He is mildly lame in his right hind leg, perhaps inflammation from an old injury he exacerbated recently, which is further unbalancing him. Give him a bute and give him today off, and tomorrow, start with just walking and a little trotting—

nothing stressful. Give him a while, maybe a week before you canter again. Let me see him again in six weeks."

OK. Nice to know what's going on. Sure, thank you, Doctor, I'll do just that. $425.

And I did. I buted. I groomed. I petted. I walked and then I trotted. I could ride him up to twenty minutes. If I rode him longer than that, he bucked me off. By now, my resting heart rate was about eighty-four, and I was developing a tremor in my hands.

There was an animal communicator who would sporadically waft by the barn, a large blonde woman with bright beads and a couple of rings with semiprecious stones the size of gnocchi. One day, when she was around, I asked for a reading. We walked down to Poker's paddock where he had begun to look plump and glossy, and Meredith began her reading. I thought it was quite wonderful that she could read him without even a momentary pause in her nonstop narrative of herself, her sister, her clothing, her animal cards . . . nothing in particular. She never stopped talking and never talked about Poker.

Suddenly and without preface, she announced, "He doesn't like his name. He thinks 'Poker Joe' sounds like 'Pokey Joe,' and he always tries his best so he doesn't like that name." OK. I'll change his name. She also thought he had had an accident at some time in his brief past (he was only eight) involving sliding down a steep hill. I thought, OK, maybe that's how he hurt his hind leg. I paid her, she talked about a "naming ceremony" she would be happy to perform for me, and I said I'd think about it.

In the meantime, I quickly set about finding a new name for my horse. I wanted a name that invoked beauty, strength, love, precious. I have always liked early English and Celtic culture and language, so I searched the net for Celtic names, medieval names, and such like. I came up with *Eoworth*, an old English word for "handsome one." Then, calling to my own cultural history, I wanted a Hebrew or Yiddish word that would be powerful and loving. I came up with the word we use to describe the tall candle on the menorah: the *Shammes*. It means "teacher" or "leader" So he became Eoworth Shammes. I called him Shammes.

Six weeks passed and even with his new name I was still getting bucked off. Dr. Amery returned. The problem was getting worse: Not only was Shammes's back sore, his lameness went from a 1 to a 3 on a scale that goes to 5 for "can't walk on it." The doctor did some acupuncture—$60 for the barn call, $375 for the acupuncture. He suggested an ultrasound. We set it up—$120 for the barn call (another horse had split it with me last time) and $625 for the ultrasound. Nothing. Another two months. I keep getting bucked off. Maybe some more chiropractic care—$120 for the barn call, $300 per session.

I started trying different saddles. English saddles, western saddles, endurance saddles, treeless saddles (definitely no). I went through about twenty-five saddles.

I started having nightmares. Desperate to get someplace and running through water over my waist. I would wake up shaken, heart racing.

Shammes was not only un-rideable; he started getting mad. Pain will do that to a person. He started pulling back when I tried to lead him up to the barn. "Get tough with him," friends said. If had he been a sound horse, that would have been good advice. One day, he resisted me and I lunged at him and smacked his butt. "You will NOT defy me!" I roared. Shammes set back stunned. He followed me meekly into the ring, and I started to lunge him.

He started out at a trot and then he reared up and started bucking in the circle around me. I was terrified, but I could not escape. I was in the middle, and whatever way I moved, he could catch me if he wanted, and I had given him reason to want to. I had no choice but to let him buck it out, terrified at 1,100 pounds of fury catapulting around attached to me by ten feet of line and this time, when he stopped I didn't even try to ride him.

I called Dr. Amery again. He suggested nuclear scintigraphy, available at a horse hospital just over the border in Connecticut. They would inject him with a radioactive material, tranquilize him, and image his entire body. He would be in quarantine for the next thirty-six hours, as he was radioactive and the material had to flush out of his body through his urine, which was collected and disposed of as hazardous waste—$2,300.

The scan showed nothing we hadn't already known. The three vertebrae right under the rider's seat were inflamed, the vertebrae almost "kissing." They suggested cortisone injections into the discs between those vertebrae. We tried it. I forgot how much that cost. I gave Shammes the day off. Then I tried to ride him again. It went OK . . . for twenty minutes. Then he bucked me off.

It was now about a year after the proud day I brought my first horse home from the program. I was a wreck after this year of punishment. My stomach would twitch and I'd feel an almost continuous pressure on my sternum. I forced myself to go to the barn every day. My legs would shake when I went to get my horse. I was using an herbal tranquilizer (Rescue Remedy) every day. I was hitting the Xanax pretty heavy once I got home. I was still on antidepressants. This was not the way it was supposed to have worked out.

Dr. Amery came yet again to the barn. He felt. He listened. He considered. He checked his notes. He sighed. Then he turned to me and said, "I'm very sorry to have to tell you this, but I can't think of anything else to try. There's nothing else I can do. You've done everything for this horse that can be done. I have to say that this is never going to be a safe horse to ride."

But . . . but, he's my horse, I silently wailed. I fell against Shammes's chestnut neck and cried.

What Happened
with Shammes

When I could speak again, I asked Dr. Amery if he had any
ideas about what to do with Shammes. He was only nine, and
while he couldn't be ridden, he could live quite comfortably in
a field for perhaps the next twenty years. I knew it would be
immoral to put down a horse like that, although it was certainly
an option. Scary to have such power of life and death over an
animal as large and as very much alive as a horse. Dr. Amery
suggested that perhaps one of the veterinary schools would consider taking him for its herd. Schools keep horses to give students the opportunity to practice techniques on a real animals:
injections, flex tests, etc. He said he would e-mail me some
contacts.

However, an even better option presented itself. By this time,
I had been volunteering at a local horse rescue for a couple of
years. One of the wealthier residents of my town had a thousand-
acre farm and had donated fully five hundred acres of some of
the most expensive land in Dutchess County for use, in perpe-

tuity, as a horse sanctuary. It was run by a remarkable and modest young woman, who at times supervised close to 140 damaged, abused, or just overworked equines, mainly from the track. The next time I went up for my volunteer time, with tears in my eyes, I asked her if she would take Shammes. "Of course I will!" she said, unhesitatingly. (This was before the financial meltdown of 2008, when the population swelled with the numbers of horses people could no longer afford to keep, so the timing was fortunate for Shammes and me.) I hired a trailer, had Shammes groomed and bathed—looking better than he ever had in his life I expect—and we headed off to the sanctuary.

I knew which of the fields he was to be released into. I often helped distribute grain in that pasture, which held about twelve to fifteen geldings. We pulled up to it with the hired rig and leveled out the trailer. I opened the tailgate and guided Shammes as he carefully stepped backward onto the dirt road. He looked around with attention, but without distress. He could undoubtedly smell horses so he knew he was not alone.

I opened the gate, led him in, and with a final caress of his muscular neck, I slipped off the halter and let him go. He hesitated, looking at me, as if to say, *Are you sure?* I nodded yes. Then he started walking from feeder to feeder, just making sure if there was anything good to eat left in them; then, from manure pile to manure pile, sniffing, seeing if there was anyone he knew. He gave a final look back at me, and then started walking away up the slight hill that led to the rest of the pasture. Then, he stopped, his head shot up. A horse appeared in the distance! He neighed. The horse neighed. He started to trot and soon was running to meet the horse, who had started running to him, and then another horse, and another horse, and soon the herd was running down to meet him as he ran up to meet them and they met in a hurly burly of whinnies and dust and *Hello! And*

Shammes and me, the day I took him to the horse
sanctuary

who are you? And soon Shammes and another horse were grooming each other and then the whole herd took off in a celebration
of new freedom with Shammes's chestnut head high above the
bay sea of horses around him, eyes bright, mane flying, and I
thought that this was no less than that good horse deserved for
as hard as he tried, through all his pain, to do his best.

I went back to the barn and sat down during a break with
Debbie. We had a cigarette. Debbie is a compassionate and per-
ceptive woman, and a tremendous lot passed between us in the
course of that smoke without ever having to say anything in
words. Then I said out loud, "I gotta get another horse." Debbie
nodded, and when she offered to help, I didn't hesitate to accept.

Nifty

There was a horse dealer in the nearby town of Millbrook whom Debbie knew pretty well. She knew some people who had gotten horses from him. We got in her truck and headed to Petey Mackey's.

Things were pretty busy at Petey's; he's got a couple of sale barns and wranglers were riding and leading horses back and forth. Deb told him what we were looking for, and we took a tour of the barn. Some nice-looking horses . . . but . . . that one too young, that one too small, that one too big. Then, in a dark and sort of damp stall, we saw a cute little bay quarter horse. We took him out. He was sweet, four going on five, well bred, good looking. Papers and everything. One of the wranglers got on him and started riding. Looked OK, but of course, those guys could ride a pterodactyl and look good. Pablo, one of the wranglers, told me he was good solid little horse, not afraid of anything, and they even roped off of him. Roped a llama, in fact! They called him the Llama Horse.

I got on him and rode around the ring. He was very nice. Obedient, willing, nice gaits. Debbie rode him. She thought so, too. I took him out of the ring and went on a short trail ride on him with one of the wranglers. He was fine. She pulled ahead; he was fine standing still as she rode away. He was fine riding away when the other horse stood still. I came back and smiled at Debbie. "I like him!" I said.

We arranged that I could come back every day for a week, ride the horse around, and see what I thought. I liked him better every day. Finally, I decided to take him home. I had bought my first papered quarter horse. His name was Nifty. And it suited him.

This was about August 2007. He was a well-broke little fella, could turn on the forehand and on the hindquarters, leg-yield, side-pass, all kinds of fancy stuff. First time out on the trail with my friends, he pulled a little rear, but it was all so new to him, I just leaned forward and put slack in the reins, and he did just

Me and Nifty

fine. "You handled that well," one of my riding buddies said. Pride filled my chest with cotton candy.

We had a wonderful autumn. It was true, he spooked at nothing, and we went out with friends for long rides every day. His coat got glossy with my diligent brushing; his mane and tail grew gratifyingly long and thick. This was heaven. I was congratulating myself as well on handling this five-year-old with such aplomb. Perhaps Shammes was truly a fluke. Perhaps I really was a good horseman, a good rider.

I started thinking about all the things I could do, with my recent training yet fresh in my mind. I changed the shanked bit to a snaffle, in general a much milder bit, because after Carl and Terry's, I knew how to train a horse, and one trained with a snaffle. At Pete Mackay's, he had been ridden with a bit that was essentially a double bicycle chain. I was trained in the humane way, and I was better than that. He did fine. Nifty and I rode far and afield, we ran and played on the extensive bridle trails of the area, and my dreams seemed to be restored.

Autumn turned into winter, and it proved to be a bad one for ice. I will ride in snow and cold, although when it gets below twenty degrees, it's not as much fun. But the ice was a real problem. Even with studs in his shoes, it was so bad there were days I couldn't even lead him from his paddock up to the barn; the road was two inches thick in glassy sheen that I could barely negotiate with Yak Trax. He, and every other horse on the place, wound up having most of that winter off. I still came out to visit him every day. I didn't have to, the barn took care of feeding him and he lived outdoors, but I still did. Every time I looked at my smart little horse, I felt proud. This was a good one.

March came, the ice melted, and I came to the barn with excitement, expecting to pick up where I had left off with Nifty, my lovely horse. I groomed him to a tee, even used Show Sheen on his mane and tail to make him beautiful. (Show Sheen is a silicone product that instantly detangles and shines. It is also slippery as wet soap.) I saddled him and being no fool, took him out on the lunge line to let him buck it out if he wanted to. He hadn't been ridden much in the last three months, and after Shammes, I wasn't taking any chances.

Nifty danced around agreeably on the lunge line as if we had never quit, picking up his gaits without hesitation. Looks like we were good to go. I brought him in, put on his bridle, and went to the mounting block. I got on the mounting block and put a foot in the stirrup, and before I could even inhale, all hell broke loose.

He bolted. Quarter horses are known for being able to explode into incredible bursts of speed from a standstill. I wasn't on yet, but determined not to get thrown again, I muscled my right leg over against the air drag and was dead center on him when he dug in his hindquarters and hit maybe forty-five miles per hour in that big riding ring. I lost my stirrups and grabbed my rein right close to the bit to haul his head around and stop him. The Show Sheen had greased the rein, and my hand slid right back to my chest without any grab whatsoever. Then, having achieved full speed, he slammed a louie, a ninety-degree turn to the left at the rail. I didn't.

I hit the fencepost headfirst and heard a *CRACK!* as my helmet split and gasps from several throats. I felt very relaxed as I hit the ground; all the sharp edges of everything I could see faded away to a comfortable gray as I heard the diminuendo sound of a horse's running hooves.

I don't know if I couldn't move, or if I just didn't want to. I was fine, except I couldn't see very well, and I couldn't call to mind the names of the friends who were now surrounding me, hauling me gently up. I was loaded in a farm cart, driven to a vehicle, and taken to Putnam Hospital Center. I was X-rayed and imaged. I had a concussion. I was fortunate. It was a Grade I concussion: I did not lose consciousness but did not know where I was or who it was who had taken me to the hospital, although I was sure it was Debbie. They kept me overnight for observation. I slowly came around but fortunately did not have any immediate need to speak cogently. I was advised against drinking alcohol anytime soon and was released. I don't remember how I got home. I don't remember the next few days. But what I did remember, what was coming back *con fuoco,* were the fear, the doubts, and the terrible anxiety of that awful year with Shammes.

It *wasn't* over. I hadn't expected this. I'd done everything right, I'd gotten educated, I got help choosing a horse, but I was still getting hurt. This was terrible. Was this what a life with horses was going to be? It would be a month before I could even think of getting on Nifty again. Even the thought was paralyzing. At some point in the day, usually about the time I'd usually go to the barn, I would find my heart starting to pump faster, and my hands start to shake.

It *was* a month. I had no pride left. I asked for help from anyone. There was a dressage instructor I had ridden with at a stable near by who occasionally taught at our barn. Catherine was a lithe woman in her fifties; she worked at a barn with the most expensive horses I had ever been close to. I caught her one day before she left, explained what had happened, and asked if she thought she could help me. "I'll try," she offered, and we set it up.

We got Nifty on a lunge line, and she started loping him around in easy circles. She was a pro, and it looked it. She stopped him, and he turned in to face her. "Western horses are trained to do that," she said, "I'm not going to penalize him for it." Off he went to the right. I was beginning to feel better already. He went around a few more times, and then it hit. Fast as lightning, he bolted, and we saw Catherine plowing the dirt with her chin for about fifteen feet before she could let go. Honest . . . she left a furrow.

We ran to her. "Oh my God! Are you all right?" from a dozen voices. She lifted herself with dignity and brushed off her jodhpurs. "I can't help you," she said. "You need a cowboy."

One of the guys who worked at the barn was a wiry Guatemalan who grew up handling horses and was great with them. He was not a large man, but he was strong as an ox. I asked him if he could help. "OK," he said, "I gonna give it a try, but le' me tell you, I wanna make him a nice horse for you, so you see me do somethin', you gotta trust me, I'm not gonna hurt him, but I'm gonna make him a nice horse for you." OK, Marcos, I understand. I trust you, Marcos. I trust you. Do whatever you have to.

Marcos is the kind of guy who's wonderful to watch. Whether he's repairing a drainage ditch, or handling a difficult horse, you can see a quiet concentration on the task at hand, his mind busy with nothing but how to do the job well and do it better. He took Nifty into the ring, once again, on the lunge line. This time, we were ready. We knew what to expect.

He eased Nifty up from walk to trot to canter. He had noticed that it was on the third time around Nifty would blow; Marcos dug in his heels and was ready. Nifty blew, Marcos held, and the lunge line busted *POP!* Marcos hit the dirt as the line broke, and Nifty tore up the ground around the ring having the best time of his life.

I tried one more time. There was a big guy who was known as a trainer and a judge and occasionally stopped by the barn to chat and keep up with what was going on in the southern

Dutchess horse world. He sometimes gave lessons at Ridgehollow. We told him the story and asked if he thought he could do anything. He thought he could, and got Nifty on a lunge line with me on his back, saying, "Don't worry, if he tries to take off, I can turn him with this and you'll be OK."

I know this is difficult to believe, but I got on, and James gave me a half hour lesson on the line with Nifty, who behaved beautifully. "OK," he said, taking me off the line. "You're fine. Go ride. Have fun!"

Thank heavens! With a grin like a pumpkin, I started trotting Nifty around the ring, working on some of the fancy maneuvers I knew he was capable of. It was going great. Until it wasn't. Some time after James left the ring, Nifty bolted again. Zero to sixy in 0.9 seconds. Dead gallop in an instant. Not wanting to crash into a fence post again, I bailed. Poorly, it turns out; Nifty's left hind hoof collided with my left shin at a full gallop, and the pain of that impact made everything go white. A grapefruit-size swelling rose almost immediately, and we went back to the emergency room. They X-rayed it. Somehow it was not broken. They didn't believe it: They took the pictures again to be sure.

After that, Debbie, Marcos, and another friend from the barn sat me down for a talk. They said that it was no reflection on my horsemanship; Nifty was just not the right horse for me at this time. They knew I was determined to be horsewoman, even if it killed me. They pointed out—that with this horse—I might succeed.

Debbie has a gift for saying even uncomfortable things in the most constructive way. Her genuine concern for me was unmistakable, and with a deep sigh, I gave in. I couldn't believe that this was the second horse in two years I was giving up. I had dreamed of a forever relationship with the horse I made mine. It just wasn't working out.

Nifty's Next Gig

So I started to look for a place for Nifty. As it happened, the woman who ran the sanctuary where I volunteered had a great idea. Given that most of these horses were rescued from racing, and that the sanctuary was affiliated with an active Thoroughbred-breeding farm, she had a lot of connections to the track. One of them was Ricky.

Ricky is an outrider. He's one of those guys you see leading out the racehorses, and "catching" them after the race has been run. As a professional rider, he is always interested in fast, well-broke horses, because he needs them to do his job. He occasionally came up to the sanctuary to get on the rescued horses Erin felt could be rehabilitated and evaluate them. He was amazing. He was not a large man, maybe five foot two or four, and he would toss his saddle on these enormous, high-strung horses, who had not been working in perhaps three months (i.e., crazy), and just swing right up. Sometimes, even in the barn aisle.

"Oh, he's a nice one!" he might say, "Lot of power, he'd be a great jumper," or "Sweet feel on her, little work and she could go someplace." He was just fearless, and knew before he got near the horse what the horse would do once he got on. "Watch out," he'd say, "this one is gonna go up. Don't want you to get hurt." He'd get on, it went up, and then he'd ride it around for a while.

So I called him, told him the situation, did not minimize the problems I had had, and asked if he'd be interested. "Yes," he said. "I am. Like to see the horse." Wow. Great. Thank heavens.

He came up to the barn a few days later with his friend, Althea, a colleague from the track, and a horse trailer. The gang at my barn had heard, and knowing Nifty's history with me, were slowly gathering around the ring. They were expecting a show. Who could blame them? So was I.

Deb brought Nifty up (I was still not walking easily), and he checked him out. Nifty was a good-looking little horse, clean, strong lines, thick mane and tail, glossy with health. "Anybody got a saddle?" he said. "You want English or western?" someone asked. "I'd prefer western, but either will do." "You need a bridle?" "No," he said. "I brought my own." He was prepared on that score. It was a conventional bit, a curb bit, but of a design meant to get and keep a horse's attention and a bit that should only be used by a skilled horseman, which Ricky certainly was. He had a lot of experience riding very "up" horses and came prepared. He called it his "heavy artillery."

He saddled and bridled Nifty, and led him into the ring. By this time, there were ten or twelve people hanging over the fence, resting a foot on the bottom rail, elbows over the top. Debbie called, "Do you want someone to hold him for you while you get up?" "Nope," he said. "I'm fine."

In the middle of the ring, with the reins sagging down to Nifty's knees, he went to get on. He stopped just as he was about to lift his foot. He perceived something invisible to the rest of us. He put his head a little closer to Nifty's ear. "WHOA," he said, with such authority that Nifty noticed. Ricky put his foot in the stirrup and swung up. Never shortening up the reins, he made Nifty do a little walk trot canter this way, and then a little that way. They glided around in rhythm together like you see on the videos. He finished it up with a reining spin to the left, a pause, and a reining spin to the right. Solid on the halt. Nailed it.

"Wow," he said. "This is a nice broke horse! But I can see where you might have had a problem with him."

Ricky took him that day. Nifty began his life as a working horse at Belmont racetrack in New York. Ricky loved him. We continued to touch base for a few months. "He's great!," Ricky would say. "He's not afraid of anything! The crowds, the flags, I even rode him through the starting gate. And . . . do you know how fast he is?" Yes, I had some idea. He told me that someone had offered him twice what he paid for Nifty, and he wouldn't sell him. But he couldn't and wouldn't let anyone else ride him. Nifty would run away with them.

So. I now had had two horses who knocked the living tar out of me. I was glad I had found good homes for them both, but that was not what I had started out to do. This wasn't quite working out as I hoped. What was I going to do now?

Well, I was going to get another horse. But maybe not just yet.

Coming Back

How on earth was I ever going to have the courage to get back on a horse? My back would never be the same after the rodeo year with Shammes. The bruise on my shin would continue to be visible for the rest of my life. I was taking anxiety medication. I was having nightmares. I was smoking compulsively. I was being torn in half. This is what I wanted to do all my life. I quit my job! I gave up my health care! Dental! My relationship with J was deteriorating because of it! And now I was so frightened of horses I couldn't even touch one. What was I going to do?

I asked everybody. I read everything. Deb suggested a wonderful book. John Lyons offered that fear was healthy: It let you know when you were out of your depth. The horse magazines ran articles on fear. Nothing helped. Finally, I asked Suzy, at the tack shop. She has a lot of experience with horses and had never steered me wrong. "What does it take to get you back, to overcome your fear of horses? I've tried everything. I've talked to everyone. I can't go back. I can't go on. What can I do? How do I come back?" "Only one thing'll do it," said Suzy. "What?" I asked, desperate. "What?" "The right horse."

She was absolutely correct.

Who I Was Before Chey

To understand what I have become, I guess I need to explain who I was before I started this experiment with horses. I had loving parents, who wanted the best for me. But I was kind of a wreck.

I was born in Queens. My grandparents on both sides left Ukraine slightly before the Russian Revolution. I guess they figured that regardless of how it turned out for the workers of the world, it was unlikely to get better for the Jews. They settled in Brooklyn, where my parents were born. The only one of my grandparents I ever knew was my mother's mother, Malke. Mom was the youngest of six, of whom five survived. Grandma was very, very old when I met her, and died when I was about six. I understand from older cousins that Malke was a martinet, ferociously demanding, and all the kids were terrified of visiting her. This was the environment my mother grew up in. I knew only an old woman who couldn't speak English. She would grab for me when we went to visit at the nursing home. I would twist out of her grasp.

Mom and Dad met at the bungalow colony the Brooklyn gang would go to on the summer weekends. They grew up during the Depression and married after World War II. Mom wore a wedding dress; Dad wore his uniform. When, late in their marriage, my parents got the house in Rego Park, Mom cherished it and kept it meticulously. She took pride in her housekeeping, an art eschewed by both of her daughters. She loved clothes and shopped well. She was a mighty snappy dresser on an admirable budget. By the time I was born, Dad was selling insurance in Bedford Stuyvesant, a very rough neighborhood in Brooklyn.

Dad was a kind and gentle man. He worked five and a half days a week. He had a heart condition, and he was always tired. When he was home, he rested. He took me to the riding stables on Sundays, where I would use my babysitting money to rent a horse for an hour in Brooklyn and Queens. We would stop at a diner on the way; he would have coffee and a bialy, I would have hot chocolate and a toasted corn muffin. It was what I lived for: my hour on a horse on Sunday, the morning with Dad. The antihistamines I had to take in order to be around horses lasted exactly an hour. And as Dad said, when I came back after my hour, I would be just starting to melt. I would tell Dad all about my ride as we drove home, snorting and dabbing with tissues as my allergy really kicked in. Then he would sit in his recliner listening to his beloved opera records on the Tonfunk. I would sit on the floor and listen with him and ask him to explain things to me. He always did, until he got sick, and then he got too tired. That is my happiest memory, other than the summers Mom and Dad sent me to Rawhide Ranch. As I recall, that was about a hundred campers and 150 horses. I was on every crew and detail, and went out into the pastures to be with the horses after they were turned out at night. I was in heaven.

Mom . . . well, my poor Mom. She kept a clean house, a kosher home, changed the sheets every week, held a full-time job, and still had a hot meal on the table for the four of us every night, except Sundays when Dad would get pizza or Chinese. We didn't appreciate it.

Dad died in 1970, a few years after we got the house and just before their twenty-fifth wedding anniversary. He was fifty-four; Mom was fifty-three, my sister was twenty-one, and I was sixteen. When Dad died, Mom took over his insurance business and still continued working at her old job. She held on to the house in Rego Park, and neither my sister nor I suffered any economic privation from the loss of our dad. Mom stopped keeping a kosher home, but made the feasts for the Jewish holidays and had all the local family over to her house to partake of them, a number that declined over the years.

All she ever wanted was to be a housewife and a mother. My mother had no priority greater than the health and happiness of her children. Unfortunately, the way she went about ensuring that proved to be unfortunate for me. I remember a time when I would dance and sing around the living room to the delight of all observers, proud and happy, the little darling. Then, things changed. I guess a time came when Mom figured the best thing she could do for me was to tell me everything I did wrong. So, wanting the best for me, she did.

It turned out there was a tremendous lot I was doing wrong. How I dressed, how I spoke, how I opened and closed doors. How I vacuumed. How I dusted. I tried to help my mom but I never, ever, ever did anything right. Even boiling water for tea: Whatever burner I chose for the kettle would be the wrong one. Even if it was explained to me on Tuesday that this was the correct burner to boil water on, by Friday that would have changed, and I could never catch up with the rules. The weight of unrelenting failure had begun to crush long before Dad died. Afterward, I just shut down more and more. I thought less and less of myself. It was only natural that in days to come I accepted people who didn't value me, who treated me carelessly, who dismissed me, because after all, these people treated me just like my mother did. So, they must be right. Right?

I found comfort in physical activity, so I would go to the schoolyard up the street and run. It angered my mother. "What the hell you doing that for? What are people going to think?" I was eleven years old, running around a schoolyard. What *were* people going to think?

Then, it was not just how I did things. It was who I was. Pick up your feet when you walk. Get that look off your face. What are you doing that for? I remember once she burst in upon me on the toilet. "What are you doing in here?" she snarled. I became afraid to even breathe around her. "What's the matter with you? I just can't teach you anything."

I was not a resilient kid. Extroverted as a child, I grew quieter, hoping to fly below the radar. I began to hide, to avoid the criticism. It didn't work. The criticism had taken root in my head and had begun to grow on its own. I developed an eating disorder, and I was profoundly ashamed.

I had few friends my own age, I was not interested in the things other kids my age were, and so I hovered just outside the cliques at school. I cut out pictures of horses, drew horses, watched a lot of television, mostly westerns.

By the time I was entering my teens, I was pretty well crushed. I had only my dreams of horses. She couldn't get into them. I'm sure it was not as Dickensian as that, but that is the way I recollect it. Something in me was spinning, and every snarl made it spin faster. I was racing inside all the time, knowing beyond any question that it was only a matter of time before I'd disappoint again and every time; it just crushed me. "I can't teach you anything."

I have heard mental health professionals say, that what happens in the first four years of your life is more important in shaping your character than what happens in the next forty. From my own experience, I believe that is true. Since I received this kind of treatment from my mother, when the world treated me similarly, it made sense. I never stood up for myself because I simply thought there was no reason to, since anyone else must know better than me. I got into exploitative relationships, worked twenty-hour days, and through holiday weekends, and took the abuse of overstressed egomaniacs because, after all, if I was worth anything, I wouldn't have had to work that hard, I wouldn't have gotten the number wrong, I would have made the call or stopped the check or whatever. I figured it was all I was entitled to expect from life, so I better get used to it.

My heart began to clutch at the idea of being around Mom. I felt horribly guilty. After all, I knew she loved me and she did so much work to keep the house nice and feed us well, but what I felt was more like hatred and that just couldn't be right, so I must have been just terribly, terribly wrong. Just like Mom was always saying. The something in me that spun was spinning faster and faster. I felt I just couldn't take much more of this, and I had no idea what I could do about it. She was right, of course, no question. There must be an answer to this. *Think! Think! You're so stupid! You can't learn anything! You're worthless! Worthless! Worthless!* That's why she has to yell at you so much! This completely consumed me, day and night. The only time I got any relief from the pressure was when I was running . . . or eating.

But I was a smart kid. Everyone said so. One day, I figured

70

out a way to finally get her approval. I got all the family's shoes and settled down in the basement with my dad's shoe polishing kit and went to work. Nailed it this time, I just knew it.

Mom called down from the top of the steps, "What are you doing down there?" "I'm polishing the shoes!" I called back, big smile on my face.

"*Psht!*" she exclaimed. "I can't believe the way you waste your time!"

I was floored. I sat there, shoe on my left hand, buffer in my right, and I felt completely erased. There was no hope. I turned to prayer. Please, God. I'll do anything, anything. Just tell me what I have to do. Please. Please. God never answered.

I left home at seventeen to go to college, and never returned to live there. Mom was so hurt that both of her daughters were in such a rush to get out. It must have been so painful for her. We were so disappointing.

I am sure that that was what was behind what she told me when I was in my fifties. Our relationship had changed. Thirty-five years on my own had given me the distance to forgive, and enabled me to begin to recognize what she had accomplished under more challenging circumstances than I had ever had to face. She took responsibility for everything she became involved in. When it appeared grandchildren were not in the offing, she became active in Hadassah, became president of her group, and became an *ima* (an honorary "grandmother" to a child in Israel, providing money and support). We became friends, and I had begun to look forward to our weekly visits. I think she knew her time was coming, and there were some things she wanted to clear up. "You know, it's all right with me that you and your sister never had a family," she said to me one day. "It really wasn't worth it."

As for me, I was well prepared to commence upon a

decades-long course of depression, anxiety, addictive and destructive behaviors in the vain search for relief from the by now permanent sneer in my head. Because I was so intelligent, I felt higher demands could and should be placed on me. My failure to meet even the most basic expectations meant I had no right to expect . . . well anything, let alone love or joy. I was always seeking the approval of that one person, any person, who would make it OK for me to live. I idolized easily. Naturally, as I matured, this strategy led me into a lot of relationships with people who were inclined to take advantage of my needs. The man I married, who had won me over with his attentive charm, proved to be a gigolo. I got into several inappropriate relationships and a few with married men. I was drinking much too much. I was meeting men who are happy to encounter drunken women. One of the guys I brought home dropped something heavy as he was taking off his coat. It was a gun. I got scared.

I had spent about fifteen years trying to be an actor. I did like the theater, and the world of ideas, but what I really wanted was to be someone else. I left college in 1973 during my sophomore year to be with the guy I would eventually marry, and because I was accepted into the Light Opera of Manhattan. They put me into every show that coincided with my schedule. Once, Robert Sherman of The Listening Room on WQXR came, and I got to meet him. Twice, we were invited to WQXR to do concert performances, once of *Pinafore* and once of *The Pirates of Penzance*.

But that was pretty much it. I never did anything as good again, except for the role of Buttercup in the Mansfield Festival Theater, and that was more of a favor a friend did for me. Ten years after I got my Equity card, I wrote my phone number on the back of it to give to a waiter I hoped would call.

But of course. How could I expect to be good at anything? I

could just get drunk, which made it easier to imagine the drunk I was with cared about me, and that gave me a little bit of comfort. Things went from bad to worse. I had started smoking. For a wonder, I avoided heavy drugs. My mind was already almost out of control, and I didn't want to chance anything that would make it worse. I was depressed and so horribly lonely that I couldn't live with it. I was abusing food.

That spiral was like gravity, accelerating over time. I feared everything, and all I sought was release from the criticism now inside my head. Being a waitress was not that demanding, and being a wastrel did not keep me from earning a living. But it got harder and harder to stay alive.

Life took so much energy. There was the internal voice excoriating me for every action, for every failure to act, for every thought I had about every action and for every reaction to every thought. It sneered at what I felt, and ridiculed what I wanted until I didn't even know what I wanted, except I knew I loved horses. But they were as far away from possible as walking on the moon. There was no release, except for the moments of substance abuse, and my shame at that was unendurable. This war upstaged everything else, consuming every waking moment. And far from finding relief in sleep, my failures were merely amplified into horrible dreams, where I wound up screaming endlessly into a silent, uninterested world.

One day, I couldn't take it anymore. I was in my late twenties. I was a failure at everything. What was the point? No one will ever love me. How could they? Even I despised me. I was living in a little Manhattan apartment, four hundred square feet with two barred windows facing a brick wall some forty feet away. I walked to the corner of it that served as a kitchen and picked up the carving knife with my right hand, and positioned it over my left wrist. I knew you were supposed to cut the long way, not across, if you really wanted it to work. I needed a shorter knife. I put the carving knife down and looked for the paring knife. There it was. I slid it out of its holder. My basilic vein looked bright blue and was easy to find. I pressed the tip of the knife on it, wondering how hard I'd have to push.

Then, a thought occurred to me. If someone as nice as me wants to die, there has to be something wrong.

I hesitated, and then I put the knife down.

Reaching Out

I'd met Dr. Weidner through singing around 1978, a few weeks before I tried killing myself. A friend had gotten a role in *The Ballad of Baby Doe*, and we were celebrating by spending an evening with his singing coach, for which we all paid a modest fee. The coach would accompany each of us on a tune, and then offer his insights into how we might deliver it better. There were about eight of us—a complete jumble of age, race, and sex (and in New York City in particular, there were often more than two). This older man was among us. We chatted a bit. I decided that given the way he spoke (i.e., logically) he might be a scientist of some kind. I was always interested in science. We wound up sitting together at the diner we all went to after. Turns out he was a shrink, a psychologist. "Funny," I said. "I was just thinking I could use some help." "Well, I'd be happy to work with you," he said. "No, I couldn't. I'd be in bed with you in a minute." He wasn't fazed. "I would be happy to recommend some excellent women therapists." "Thanks. I'll think about it."

The night of my aborted suicide, I called him. I needed help, I said, and I couldn't wait. "Let's start right now then," he said. "What's going on?"

I started therapy. Twice a week. Tuesday and Thursday.

Turnaround

Theater didn't work out; marriage didn't work out, either. OK then, if I couldn't have love, I wanted money. As much as I could make. I thought about what the most overpaid profession I had any chance of entering might be. It was 1984, so the answer was Wall Street.

Not only was I just divorced. I was also on the verge of losing all my college credits. It had been more than ten years since I dropped out to join Light Opera of Manhattan and be with the guy I later married.

Baruch was the obvious answer: It was local; it was affordable. I was paying for this myself, after all. I applied in January. The only course open was macroeconomics, and I didn't even know what that was. I thought about waiting until the spring to enroll, but a voice inside said, *No, if you don't go back to school right now, you never will.* I was afraid it might be true, so I enrolled in the night school and proceeded to study economics and finance. I got a full-time job as a secretary in a financial firm (thank heavens, I could type), to get practical experience in the field. I commenced having an affair with my boss. He was the most attractive man I'd ever met to that date, and it made the job a little more interesting. When I graduated from CUNY in 1987, he knew he couldn't do anything for me, and that I would never leave him, so he fired me. Three months' severance, and I could use the office to find another job. "You'll hate me now, but someday, you'll thank me." He was right. I happened to be pregnant at the time. By him. For the second time. He knew. But what really hurt . . . so was his wife. She had hers.

Mom knew nothing about that part, just that I went back to school and got a useful degree. As I pounded my way through the asymptotic pressure and the tooth-cracking anxiety of being an analyst on Wall Street, she was, finally, proud of me. However, I was a wreck. Dr. Weidner had seen the danger signs of accelerating anxiety and deteriorating self-esteem, and feared suicide might be looking attractive again. He referred me to a psychiatrist for medical assistance. I started with the classic, Prozac, and over the course of the next twenty years would also sample Effexor, Lexapro, Paxil, Wellbutrin, Zoloft, and I'm sure some I've forgotten. They would work for a few months and then I'd sink again, so he'd switch me to something else. By this time, I was working in finance, as a professional. Anxiety became paralyzing. Xanax, tobacco, and alcohol did the trick most of the time. Sometimes, in the early morning, Dr. W would talk to me for two hours, because I was too anxious to even get out of bed and face my job. And after our regular sessions in the evenings, I would return to work where I'd typically work until 1:00 or 2:00 a.m. Unless we were busy, then I'd work longer.

I lived in a constant panic. But I was intelligent, articulate, and well groomed, and I hid it all marvelously. When I "auditioned" for a real job in finance, I knew how to play the role.

Wall Street

I got a job in the mergers and acquisitions department of Merrill Lynch in the World Financial Center on Vesey Street. Wall Street personified. Most analysts were twenty-one. I was thirty-four. My first day on the job was Thursday, October 15, 1987. I was shown into a bullpen, assigned a cubicle with a computer, received an HP-12C calculator, and a volume of *Using Lotus 1-2-3*, which was about six inches thick. That was it. That was my training. I was on the job. *BAM!* There was no warm-up. We were on live deals that afternoon.

Perhaps you remember what happened on Monday, October 19, 1987. In four days, I was already past my capacity in computer modeling. Around about 3:30 p.m., the perimeter aisles started filling up with people. You couldn't help but notice, even lost deep in cyberspace. At that time, it was B.B. (Before Bloomberg) and B.C.I. (Before Common Internet): So major financial firms like mine had Quotrons placed every thirty or forty feet, within ready view, which showed the market's activity on a computer-size monitor in real time. I got up to join the crowd staring at the amber digits on the screen representing the Dow. By about 3:45 p.m., it was ticking down a point or two *every second*. I looked up at a managing director standing just behind me, an old-timer set to retire this week. "Is this . . . usual?" I asked. "Nope" he said. "It's not."

By the end of that day, the market as represented by the Dow lost 508 points, 23 percent of its value, $500 billion in market capitalization evaporated in minutes. It was the largest one-day decline in history, *including* the Crash of 1929. At that, we had it easy. Markets in Asia and Europe crashed by as much as 60 percent. In Iceland, the decline was 77 percent. The panic was unbelievable. Volume in the New York Stock Exchange that day was 604 million shares, versus an average volume of 141 million in 1986, and the tape was two hours behind. In those days, stock and bond transactions were done on paper. It took months to catch up. Brokers slept under their desks for days.

Well, that was my introduction to Wall Street. Catastrophe. Would the world ever recover?

Sure it would.

Although it would be hard to top my first days on Wall Street, the next eighteen years were to be no less dramatic. Had I the slightest competence with numbers, I might have been excited to be involved with deals that hit the papers every day. Not even multimillion dollar deals. Multi*billion* dollar deals. I had to pass the Series 7 (an SEC requirement); I was fingerprinted at the police station on East 51st Street (a requirement for anyone dealing in securities). I was working eighteen to twenty hours a day, on several deals at once, and there was no excuse for not having anyone's work done on time. Merrill served dinner every night at about 8:00 p.m. We analysts would fill up a tray and take it back to our computers. Merrill provided a car service for us, because we were generally going home at 3:00 or 4:00 a.m. I was doing pretty much the same work throughout my career, although the responsibilities and expectations expanded with time. It would go as follows.

Company A wants to buy Company B. We needed to do two sets of "comps": company comparables and transaction comparables. If we didn't know much about the businesses Company A and B were in, we had to learn in a hurry. Then we had to find five or six other companies in the same lines of business as A and as B. If Company A had multiple lines of business (like Halliburton or Bechtel) we would have to find comparable companies in each line of business. We would input three to five years' of financial history for each of the companies, typing them digit by digit into the computer model we created for each deal. We would dredge up these numbers from their 10Ks (annual reports) and 10Qs (quarterly reports), which we would order from the library downstairs. They would print them from the SEC archives to which they had access (Internet was just starting, and among the first resources available were Nexus, a searchable database for published news, Lexus, ditto for legal research, and the SEC archives). We needed income statements, balance sheets, cash flow statements, notes. This was not just input. These financial models had to flow, with the changes in the income statements and balance sheets generating the cash flow statement, which was what we were really interested in. Loans get paid back from cash, not from income. "Income," as we were to learn, is a highly manipulable number. Inventory accounting methods, tax strategies, currency exchange rates, accelerated depreciation, and amortization: There were lots of ways, all kosher, all within Generally Accepted Accounting Principles, or GAAP, that could be employed to accelerate or delay income.

Often, accounts were combined or segregated in ways not obvious to a number aphasiac like me, so this was an agonizing process. Of course, as we went through the fifteen or twenty sets of financial statements (for each entity), we also needed to read all the notes, which might explain an unusual handling of some account, or a tax treatment or loss carryforward that had an important impact on cash flow. Was the company international? How did foreign accounting standards and currency exchange rates impact reported results? Have there been any extraordinary events? Were accounting standards used that gave a more favorable treatment to some aspect of operations? Was the company using accelerated depreciation? Then we had to compare the operations of each of the competitors over time with the subject company, on an "apples to apples" basis.

Then we had to learn about the respective industries. In what stage of the growth cycle was the industry, what was the market, what economic, environmental, technological, financial events would impact the industry, who were the market leaders, was there a lobbying presence, was there political interest in supporting or depressing the industry. Who were the important analysts, what did they say about the companies and the industry. What did the rating agencies think?

Then we had to create a cash flow model, modeling company performance for the term of the loan (usually seven years). God help you if you couldn't justify every one of the thousands of numbers that went into it. We generally did three scenarios: expected, worse, and worst. We needed to get a sense of how much value could be eroded before it had an impact on the company's ability to repay whatever debt we were thinking of lending to the transaction. Then we had to evaluate how and if the structural protections in the loan might preserve us, how they compared to the structure of the other "tranches" of debt on the balance sheet, and, if all else failed, we would have done a "liquidation analysis" to get a feel for what we could "reasonably" expect to recover from the liquidation of the various classes of assets, after more senior obligations, if any, were addressed. There were two types of liquidation we analyzed; an "orderly liquidation," and the other kind, referred to as a "fire sale." But we weren't done yet.

Then, the acquisition comps. The underlying rule in finance is: *A thing is worth whatever anyone else will pay for it.* So we had to dig up and analyze as many other similar transactions in the industry as we could to determine the multiples at which the target was acquired; how many times EBITDA (Earnings Before Interest, Taxes, Depreciation, and Amortization); what was the resulting leverage (Total Debt/EBITDA, Senior Debt/EBITDA); what was the interest coverage, interest + principal repayment coverage, interest + principal plus maintenance CAPEX ("capital expenditure") coverage. If the going rate was an acquisition price of 5.2x EBITDA, and yours was 5.8x, that might still be OK, but it might not. It was my job to evaluate any factors that might support higher leverage than average, or less.

There was a marketing component to this metric, as well. Investors (i.e., the people who bought stock) want as much debt as possible, because leverage (i.e., debt) increases the return on equity.[3] Lenders want as little debt as possible, because the less money a company has to pay out for interest, and the less other debt there is to repay, the more cash there is to pay the interest and principal on the debt you are thinking of lending.

Then, we had to analyze the structure of the deal. What was

---

3. For example: If a company is capitalized with $50 in debt and $50 in equity, and earns $10, the return on equity is 10/50 or 20 percent. If it is capitalized with $90 in debt and $10 in equity and earns $10, the return on equity is $10/$10 or 100 percent. Which would you rather have?

the term of the loan, how senior was it, what protections did we have against performance that was below plan, what was the security, under what conditions could we get more security, how good was this security, what was the limit on CAPEX, how about acquisitions or divestitures, what was the interest rate, under what conditions could the rate increase or decrease, what was the interest rate based on (it was usually LIBOR, the London InterBank Offer Rate)? How would the credit agreement be amended? What would be the governing law? The credit agreements usually ran between 100 and 150 pages. I would have to analyze it and write a summary.

Then I had to write it all up in a credit proposal of some fifteen to twenty pages, with cash flow projections and exhibits adding another forty to fifty pages to provide the basis for every word I said, and submit it to the next level up. And then, at the credit committee, they got to interrogate me. If they ask a question and you don't have the answer, you feel like an egg in a skillet.

And so on. And at any point in this process, someone might burst into my cubicle and need a fast answer on another deal, some detail that I could never recall, immersed as I was in whatever deal I was on that moment.

At first, it was three weeks from bank meeting to commitment date. Since for most of my time in finance, I worked for foreign banks, which meant two weeks to give head office a week to review the proposal. Later on, it became two weeks, so I had one week to do all that. Toward the very end, there would be a junior person to help with the cash flow projections. But the responsibility for the deal was mine.

Then, after the deal was done, I was responsible for monitoring it, reading all the financial statements the company filed with the SEC, charting its compliance with the plan, and writing quarterly reviews of the company and the deal, with recommendations as appropriate. I might have eight to twelve portfolio companies. 10Qs might run fifteen pages, 10Ks much longer. So that meant I had to read 120 to 500 pages and absorb all that information in a matter of days to be able to make my recommendations. Should we stay in the deal? Should we sell out? Sometimes we would be heading toward bankruptcy. Should we take a reserve? Then things really got hot.

It was never less than overwhelming. I learned to work as hard as I could, as fast as I could, as long as I could, and there was always the next deal. I needed to know if anything happened, anywhere, that had anything to do with any of my deals. Or else. I was seeing my therapist twice a week, returning to work after our sessions. I would call him frequently, to get me through quotidian crises. My medications were ramping up in dosage, and I still needed to get drunk anytime I had a window of a few hours to recover. I smoked constantly, until it was outlawed in office buildings, and then, just whenever I could. I lived in a war zone in my head. Not only that: I whipped myself for my miseries, thinking, I was free, white, and twenty-one, born in America in the twentieth century to parents who actually wanted me. What the hell was my problem? I figured if I could just punish myself sufficiently, it would stop. It never did, and I never stopped trying.

There was no relief even in the few hours I'd have to sleep. My dreams were full of missed flights and lost numbers and running through molasses to get somewhere you absolutely had to be long before. Why did I stick with it? There was no alternative. Joy was out of the question for me.

But there was the money. I made it. I didn't spend it. And there was Mom. At last, I was doing something that pleased her. I was (in her eyes) a successful businesswoman with an important job and a real title. And nice clothes. She bought me a gold bracelet when I made vice president. She was so proud of me.

Mom. Toward the end, I was able to forgive her. I was able to recognize what it was she intended versus what I got. And when I did that, I began to see her as a whole person. My mom, for all her flaws, had virtue and compassion; she lived in difficult times and always tried to give back more than she took. For the last bit of her life, we became friends. I'd go out once a week and we'd have lunch or dinner. Mom was in her eighties by now, and some things were becoming more difficult, like traveling. But she still loved shopping, still looked sharp. So, hey, Mom, I have Monday off, how 'bout we go to Queens Center and look at the stores? I was actually beginning to look forward to the time I'd spend with her. Then she died.

But . . . back to horses.

I Get Help

Celia is a name around here in Dutchess County. She is large (about six feet and more than two hundred pounds) and intimidating; her size alone would do it but the energy that comes from her is memorable. She is a no-nonsense kind of person. Not everyone is ready for Celia, (I just flashed on Jack Nicholson leering, "You can't handle the truth!") She can be blunt to the point of being tactless or, sometimes, even cruel. She really doesn't care about hurting your feelings. She considers it "toughening you up." If you are sensitive, you'd better work with someone else. She is not for everyone, but until now, she had always been kind to me.

She is maybe five or six years younger than I was, which is to say she was in her fifties at the time, which was late summer of 2008. She will tell you she has been training horses since she was about ten and teaching adults to ride since she was about fourteen. She is married to an old horse trader, who makes a nice living as a welder, and in any other way he can. He always has something to sell, tack, horses, hardware. "Do yourself a favor, mortgage your house and buy this horse!" is a favorite phrase. He has a small property, and they keep a few horses. He has made it possible for her to compete in the National Cutting Horse Association (NCHA). She has a belt buckle (in western disciplines, a belt buckle is like a National Book Award in literature, a Pulitzer Prize in journalism). She and her husband have a nice mare out West somewhere, who has given them some nice babies. Celia will start them, then send them to a professional trainer for finishing as cutting horses.

I first met her after we bought the house in Dutchess County in 1997, when I would look for someplace to ride to prepare for my annual vacations in Wyoming. I discovered riding in Wyoming through a tour company and was absolutely hooked. I would spend my entire vacation out West, driving cattle or horses, or just joyriding, in the saddle up to ten hours a day, camping out in tents at night, and while an hour or two over a couple of weeks was hardly adequate preparation, it was something.

There was a barn, Diamond Bar C, where they specialized in cutting and where Celia often taught. She put a pair of spurs on me (oh my goodness!) and gave me lessons on a grand old cutter named C-Bar, who I later leased. He was a jackhammer. Celia loved him for that. If you could sit his trot, you could sit anything.

When I was in Suzy's asking about how get back after being murderized by horses, I mentioned some of the problems I had been having. Cordy, a local cowgirl, mentioned Celia. "She's helped me out quite a bit," she'd said. And I thought, *Hmmm. Celia.*

Celia's place was right down the road from me. I stopped by.

"Well, hello!" said Celia, offering me a hug. (Any hug from Celia is a big hug.) "How are you?"

I told her that I had made a big change in my life: I decided I couldn't wait any longer and had quit my job to pursue a life with horses. That I didn't just want to learn to ride better, I wanted to be a horseman. She seemed delighted for me.

"But," I said, "in the last two years, I. Have. Had. The. Absolute. Crap. Beat. Out. Of. Me." And now, I couldn't get close to a horse without shaking so hard I couldn't hold the lead line. "So I have a problem. I can't live without horses. But I'm scared to death of them. Can . . . can you help me?"

A glow seemed to come over this big, tough horsewoman as she smiled and bent down close to my face. "I'm so glad you came to me," she said. "Yes, I can."

So I started taking lessons from Celia in late summer 2008. The first time was at her place, on their old lesson horse, Pie. I was scared to death.

"Hi," she beamed as I ambled toward her and the horses she had tied up on the rail. "How ya doing?" "OK," I said uncertainly. "Are you afraid now?" "N-n-n-no," I lied. "Are you OK around horses on the ground?" "Sometimes." She smiled. "Do you think you can get on old Pie here?" "Yes," I said, and I went over and while she held him, I got on after about three tries. My leg wouldn't stop shaking long enough to boost me up. Then I was on. "You're not afraid now?" "Uh . . . n-n-n-no," I said. "Why is that?" asked Celia. "Because this is your horse, and I know he's broke to death!"

So Celia got on her horse Spend the Money (Money for short), and we went into her ring. "Just sit on him," she said. "Feel him. Feel him. Move with him." I began asking if my feet were right, my hands, and she said, "Don't worry about that

89

right now. Just feel the horse." And so I rode that excellent retired cutting horse, and I think the lesson lasted a couple of hours. I was tense and bracing for the fall and expecting to fall and my body was swinging and my legs were stiff and a couple of times I did something and Pie stopped on a dime.

"I'm doing it wrong!" I moaned. "Uh-uh," Celia said. "You don't get to do that. If you're doing something wrong, I'll tell you. You do not get to criticize yourself." And on we went. I wanted to stop, but Celia wouldn't let me. Sometimes Pie would slow or hesitate or swing wide and she would yell, "Don't let him get away with that! Nail him!" What? Me? Yes, me.

So, I started riding Pie at Celia's place, and she began chipping away at the granite of my fear and self-criticism over and over. I'd apologize; she wouldn't let me. I'd make excuses; she wouldn't let me. I'd ask about what I should do, and she'd say, "Stop thinking about yourself. Think about the horse." When I would worry about doing something wrong and getting hurt again, she would say, "Look at me. Nothing is going to happen to you on a horse when you are with me. I won't let it."

One thing I took away from Carl's is that when you are on a horse, the responsibility for your safety is yours alone, but there are times when you are just not ready for it. It remains a wonder to me that more people are not hurt by horses, a testament more to the kindness of horses than the wisdom of humans. But that's why there are teachers. Then, there are teachers and there are teachers. I lucked out this time. Celia has such personal power, that when she says it, you can believe it. And after a while, I did believe it.

At each lesson, she would say to me, "How are you doing?" I was still pretty scared, even though I had been on Pie a few times without getting hurt. "I'd like you to give it all to me," she'd say. "What?" I'd say. "The fear. The anxiety. Give it to me. I'll take charge of it, and if you want it, you can have it back after the lesson!" Every week, I was able to give a little more of it away. Celia is capacious, and took it all.

Our lessons didn't go by the clock. Celia would work me until I got something.

Remember those three rules?

You can't get hurt.

The horse can't get hurt.

The horse had to be calmer after the lesson than before.

Funny thing. That is just what working with Celia was like in those days. I never got hurt, and no matter how I came into the lesson, no matter what negative thinking or experiences at home or frustrations with J I brought with me, I always felt good when we were done. Another trainers' adage: *Always end on a good note, because the way you put a horse away is the way he will be when you take him out.* Yeah. Me, too. Celia put me away on a good note. But, most important for me, I began to feel safe again. After Carl's, after James "helped" me with Nifty, I didn't know what to think about trainers. But Celia was working out. She loves teaching, and she has been around horses long enough that she can tell exactly what you're doing on a horse, even if he's on the side not facing her. She can tell because she sees it in the horse. It's true. If you are tensing your right ankle or you're putting more pressure on your left sit bone than the right, the horse will move differently. Relax your back. You're tensing your butt muscles. Open your knees. Move with the horse. "I can't." "You can, and you better get used to the idea that you can, because we're gonna keep doing it until you do!"

I would ride with her at her place, on good old Pie. He had taught a lot of people how to ride, including at least a couple of actors who needed it for their roles, whom Pie treated no differently than me. He was a grand old horse, a professional, the most athletic and best-trained horse I ever rode up until then. He did not take it easy on you just because you were learning. He expected as much of you as Celia did and had been known to buck a cowboy or two off. But I believed I was safe with him and Celia. And I was.

Little by little, through the summers, the falls, the autumns, and the winters, my lessons with Celia became the highlight of my week. She seemed always cheerful, always present, 100 percent there for you no matter what issues she may have had in her own life. She pounded away at my insecurities and my self-doubt, my negativity and my self-incrimination. She could tell me more about what my mind was going through than I could articulate myself. As we worked together, my mind slowed down, my anguish receded, my confidence grew albeit infinitesimally and I began to look forward to riding horses again.

Finding Cheyenne

But I still needed a horse of my own, and no way was I going to choose another without help. That meant Celia. We heard about Jim, a purported retired cutting horse and his pony friend, Lady. He lived in a fellow's backyard in the general area. Celia came to check him out.

Storm clouds were gathering in the sky, and we could hear thunder moaning in the distance. "Let's get moving, before the rain comes." She threw her saddle on him and swung on. He was terribly out of shape, his feet were a mess, his owner had not even known that horses need to have their teeth taken care of annually, and he was not happy to be made to work. He trotted a little, picked up an unbalanced canter, and popped a few crippled bucks. She rode out the bucks, got him loping again and rode him around for a bit. Then she got off, pulled off her saddle, "We'll be in touch," she said, and we headed back to my Jeep.

"This horse has never been a cutting horse," Celia said. "His feet are so bad it may take two years of proper trimming to fix them. There is so much wrong with him it's hard to tell how much of it is related to neglected feet and how much to other physical problems. But in any case, this is not a horse for you."

I was disappointed. He'd looked OK to me. But I did not argue, I had paid for my ignorance with blood and bruises. Jim and Lady had a happy ending, though. Debbie adopted them! She got them both healthy and sound, and then found a rescue that would take them forever.

Once again, I turned to Debbie. She seemed to remember seeing a notice on the board of one the tack shops about a grade (i.e., not pedigreed or papered) horse for sale. Contact Joanne.

Joanne had run a boarding facility in Westchester but gave it up when property became too expensive. She moved upstate where she and her family and her family's horses were now. When she ran the boarding stable in Westchester, this horse was there, owned by a big guy who learned to ride from cowboy movies. The mare was a nice horse, Joanne said, but she did not respond well to the way the guy manhandled her. He would jerk her around and pound her into a run, drag her to a stop and dump her back in her pen. She objected. He started using bigger bits. She started tossing her head to evade the pain. He put a tie down on her, so she couldn't. She became hard to catch. They started leaving a halter on her 24/7. It was too tight. The guy wound up getting divorced, and one way or another (and I suspect it was the other), the horse came into the ownership of Joanne.

Joanne already had more horses than she needed. She had posted the notice on Suzy's tack store bulletin board, which is where Deb had seen it. While I was in the shop talking to Suzy about the posting, Cordy happened to be there, who had actually met the horse. She sometimes rode problem horses for people.

"I know that horse. I've ridden her. Let me tell you: You don't want this horse," she said. "She's a project. Head always up in the air. Crappy attitude. You don't want her." Oh. Well. I went to see the horse anyway.

You really didn't need any more than the scars on her face to be able to figure out her story. Her wary eye and tracking ear were unnecessary confirmation. The look in her face was a lot of things, but it was not friendly. How could you blame her? Her life so far had taught her that humans are not to be trusted— and I know from my own experience, that what you learn first counts more than what you learn later—and that it takes an awful lot of "good" to make up for even a little "bad."

The mare was what's called flaxen chestnut, a dark honey color with blond mane and tail, although the tail was kind of eaten up by ticks. She was built solid, like a workhorse, stout legs and big hooves. A little potbellied from lack of exercise. Joanne lunged her at walk, trot, canter; she picked them all up, and her legs looked straight from the front and the back. Her daughter rode the mare (in an English saddle). I got on. She stood for mounting, which at that point was almost all I cared about. I was too afraid to move. Joanne told me, she'd ridden the mare on trails and on the road, She was good with traffic, she was a levelheaded horse, and she didn't spook at much, just once, when she saw a snake, she gave a little jump. We agreed she'd come to the barn for a trial.

When Cheyenne (I called her Chey) did come to Debbie's, I was still not sure I was ever going to be able to ride a horse on my own again. I was still that scared.

Joanne led Chey out of the trailer, and I saw a powerful horse on high alert, head in the air, white surrounding her irises. "Do you want to take her?" Joanne asked. She was holding the dancing horse by the halter to restrain her. "No," I said. I showed

95

Joanne which paddock she'd go into, and Joanne brought the horse to it and released her. The horse leaped away and started snorting her way around the acre that represented her new home, prancing the way horses do when they are alarmed, which is really quite beautiful to watch if you are at a safe distance. And she did look beautiful to me, flaxen mane and tail and powerful neck arched in concern as she danced around and made acquaintance with the other horses in smell and earshot. Then she took off and comforted herself with a short bucking gallop around her field, her sturdy hooves pounding postholes into the soft ground. My heart was racing so fast I couldn't count it. I'm never going to be able to ride that.

But Joanne was calm and smiling and wished me luck, and then she turned the horse trailer around and went home. God, to have that confidence . . .

Celia came to the barn to check out Chey. Again, threw the saddle on, pushed her through her paces. The horse complied like a cranky couch potato that was unwilling to play this game. Really unwilling.

Celia halted her and spoke to me from onboard. "Well, I have to tell you, I am really not impressed with this horse. She's not built good, her stifle is too narrow, and her back's too long. She's out of shape and her attitude is lousy. She is not an athlete; she hauls herself around instead of pushing off her rear. I am not impressed."

Sigh.

But then, Celia dismounted and said, "Why don't you get on her, I'll give you a lesson on her, and we'll see."

I got on this cranky horse and did my best to listen and participate in the lesson, which lasted a couple of hours. I am sure I did not make it easy on the horse, as out of shape as she was, and as limited as I was. But after a while, when we finished the

We're both still pretty nervous.

lesson and I was still full of doubt, Celia said, "All right. We can work with this." So, when the two weeks were up, Joanne cashed my check, Chey had a new home, and I had a new horse.

Later on, Celia told me, the real reason she gave the OK was that Chey had spoken to her. What the horse told her was:

I will not hurt her.

And she never has.

97

Progress

So, I started riding Chey, taking lessons from Celia in August 2008. It was terrifically frustrating. After all the riding I had done, on the weekends, the vacations in Ireland, Morocco, and Wyoming, I was continually stunned to discover how little I could do. Apparently, "just staying on" and "riding" are not synonymous. I was working so hard and getting nowhere. I was three years into this, I took a program, and I wasn't training horses yet!

I took note of my handwriting—so fast and jagged it looked like it had been written by an Alzheimer's patient. The frantic pace of my prior life on Wall Street continued driving my horse life. It wasn't working.

I was still on antidepressants at this time. With Celia in my life, I had eased off the Xanax, a little, because I could trust Celia, and the horse was working out. But a lifetime of self-doubt continued to plague me, castigate me, for failing to become the renowned horseman I had set out to be. I couldn't help but think I had been so wrong about so many things: Shammes, Nifty, Jim, the "not-a-cutting horse" Celia rode for me while the thunder rolled. I was sooo wrong. About sooo many things. Horses were just the latest.

Debbie said it first: "You need to learn to read horses better." Yes, yes, I know, I want to! Right now! Celia said, "You are looking at horses through rose-colored glasses." Was I ever! Not just horses, either. Now that was a real tool. But what did it mean? I only knew one way of looking at things. Hoping and always wrong in the end. I began thinking about that.

I could start with Chey. When I opened my eyes, I could see, far from being a dream horse, she was anxious. She would not stand on the crossties, where we tied horses to groom and saddle. She would not allow the farrier to shoe her. In fact, the regular guy gave it a try, and informed me that he knew I'd feel bad if he got hurt, but he'd feel worse, and if I wanted to find another farrier, that would be fine by him.

Oddly enough, I wasn't afraid of Chey. She made her feelings known, and this horse's only experience with people put her on the defensive. But she never made me feel that I was in serious danger, which is saying something because that particular sense was still hyperactive in me. However, I was not getting anywhere fast. My confidence was still weak. I saw the teenagers at the barn jump on any horse, with or without a saddle, goof around over fences and at speed, and I would feel like a failure because that would have been impossible for me.

But Chey was beautiful to my eyes. As she submitted to my grooming, her bronze coat and flaxen mane began to shine, her tail was filling out, and she was warm and silky. The time we spent together in this way became a pleasure for me. And I think for her. She began to relax.

The lessons with Celia continued. I kept berating myself. She kept telling me that was not my job; it was hers. I was reverting to an old strategy, hoping that if I beat myself up enough, other people wouldn't. It never worked before, and it was a habit Celia wouldn't accept. "Stop that," she said. "Think about what to do, not what you shouldn't do."

Just like with horses. Horses don't understand "Don't." "Don't paw in the aisle." "Don't stop at the gate." They only understand "Do." "Move left" (instead of pawing). "Go faster (instead of stopping)." For horses, positive is the only way to go. For humans, we can make a choice about how to go. But among the most important lessons I learned was that positive is *always* better.

My intelligence had always been my survival tool. Oddly, now I needed to stop using my head, specifically my left brain, which had worked such overtime in banking and had developed such toxic habits as I tried to punish my way to self-respect. I had a powerful brain, but it had gotten into such bad habits that it was limiting me. It consumed me with anxiety and self-loathing. Because of it, I was totally self-absorbed, with all my psychic energy going into defending myself against what I knew would be a losing battle for perfection.

Chey was so vivid and physical. She could show me the way. But I was still so afraid, so distant. I couldn't let go. What I really needed to do—if I wanted to know horses better—was to use the other side of my brain, the side that experienced music and poetry, rhythm and balance. The thinking was killing me. But this was a horse Celia told me I could trust to teach me to feel, to be, to be a part of something. I didn't have to live only in my head. I had this horse. She could show me how to live in her world. A world of rhythm and balance. Music and poetry. Unity of mind and body.

I kept kicking myself for this not working out as I had planned. (Of course! How could it? I wasn't even living in reality.) But the way it was working out was with happy time with Cheyenne. I needed to stop thinking about where I thought I should be and be where I was. And I was so happy to be doing this now. I worked out a life where I spend time every day with my horse, and this one hadn't hurt me.

That's not so bad. Not bad at all. It's just great.

The Home Front

It was 2009: three years since I had stopped working at the bank and made the momentous decision to change my life. Horses were a start. But there was a lot more to work on: my relationship with J who bought the house with me and with the people I called friends.

Let's start with the first one: I had a very wave-form relationship with this man. From the beginning, some things didn't make sense to me. Like, his not being happy for me when I embarked on this course. You expect the person you're with to be made happy by what makes you happy. But even before, there were things that were off.

We met on a hike in the early 1990s. In my "before" period, hiking was how I sublimated my desire to be near horses. I was going on a Labor Day weekend hike and helping out the hike leader (with whom I had hiked before) by handing out and collecting releases. J came around the corner in a marine blue polo shirt, with a cup of coffee in one hand, a duffel bag and the *New*

York Times in the other. He was the handsomest man I'd ever seen close up, and I threw myself at him. He didn't mind too much.

I was on the high side of my manic cycle. Happy to be getting out of the city, happy to be hiking and running up the trails, happy to have hooked this man. I jabbered on incessantly, and he listened. I was certain this meant we were jake. We continued seeing each other, on the weekends when I didn't have to work. I would ask, "What would you like to do? What would you like to eat? What would you like to watch?" He never actually answered, but I was happy to go along with whatever he wanted to do. He seemed happy, too.

We didn't have conversations. He would just agree, or demure. He didn't talk much. In fact, he expressed no opinions. Ever. Did you like that movie? How was that restaurant? Do you like this outfit? Tell the truth, he never lied about anything. He just said nothing.

I ignored it and kept talking. Silence is assent, right? He was obviously intelligent. Yet, he did not seem to be as curious about things as I was. That was OK. I just kept talking. He showed up, and that was all I hoped for. Felt it was more than I deserved. We hiked and skied and went to the beach. We started going on vacations together.

He didn't mind my drinking, even when I got drunk, as I did pretty regularly. He didn't mind my smoking. In fact, he would rather drive with me at midnight to find a pack of smokes than talk to me. I was very confused, but he was handsome, and he behaved well. He didn't actually seem very interested in me, but he didn't leave. He didn't like touching or being touched. That was OK, whatever, as long as he didn't leave.

When, in the mid-1990s, I decided to look for a house outside of the city, he suggested, "How about I go in on it with you?" I was elated. There it was. "Would you like to get married?" I asked. "No," he said. *That's OK,* I thought. *That's OK.*

So, we started looking in September 1996 and in February 1997 he found this place and said excitedly, "We could look at a thousand more houses and never find one as nice as this!" I took an afternoon off work, and saw it, and it was nice, and I probably couldn't have made the decision by myself, because I couldn't make any decisions by myself, but I was grateful to ride on his. I was terrified of the financial commitment. Mom, as always, knew exactly what to say to inflate my fears into seismic proportions: "Jeez, do you know how much it will cost to have a house?" After a mini-breakdown and relying on what I felt had to be the superior common sense of J, we bought the house in Dutchess County. We owned it fifty-fifty.

He immediately started buying things (I shared the cost, of course), and I was flabbergasted. What's the rush? Can't we wait and find stuff that is nice? Can't we wait until we're at least there? Can't we have some kind of plan or theme or idea of what the house should look like? But he was a juggernaut, buying things at tag sales, filling the house up and more, before I felt I could even catch my breath. *Stop! Stop!* I wanted to say, *Not so much stuff! Please!* But it never came out. I was powerless, just being carried along by the tide. I had hopes of a clean, well-lit home, with beautiful things to look at with every turn of the head. Remember, I was living in a tiny New York City apartment with a bathtub in the kitchen and two barred windows facing a wall. But he did not seem to be concerned with whether colors or styles matched. He wanted the house to be full, as quickly as possible. Until it overflowed.

But it was all right. It would be all right. My time would come, I was sure of it. At some point, what I think would matter.

At first, we were just up there on weekends. I'd haul Goodwife Cozy up in the Sherpa carrier on the train. We realized we'd need a car. So I bought one, and we used it. We'd shop for food for us and the cats, and then it would be a matter of me asking what we would do and him saying "I'll think about it." I waited, until he decided what it was we would do that day, and then I did it. He'd realize some day that it was a little thoughtless to just string someone along like that; that it didn't let them make any plans of their own. He'd realize, and my time would come.

It turned out he had very different ideas about organizing a household as well. As in—none. It drove me crazy. Nothing had a "place." Spices overflowed the spice rack, so they'd find new homes by the screwdrivers. The refrigerator had no "dairy" section, "vegetable" section. If you wanted to see if we had any salad dressing, you might have to empty the entire fridge. The tools would never be where I had seen them last.

One day, we found a dining room set with four chairs by the side of the road. It was lovely. We started loading, and he said, "These are too many chairs. We don't need them." I was a little confused. Four chairs? Too many? Then one day, I wanted to make cupcakes and couldn't find those little paper cups you put in the tray. "Oh," he said, "I threw them out. I don't need them." But . . . what about *me*? *I* use them! I got worried. As a horse-person, I had a lot of leather equipment and a box of leather care stuff—saddle soap, sponges, rags. "Do you see this?" I felt I had to say one weekend, holding up the box in front of him. "This is my stuff. This is important to me. Don't discard it."

It drove me crazy. But I never questioned it and still held on. And we still took vacations together and came up to the house every weekend before I quit my job. But as I progressed with my horse, some things began to change.

Chey gave me the opportunity to ask for something and insist on getting it. It is acceptable to require something from a horse.

It was a new concept for me. As I got better at asking, she responded more quickly. Celia urged me to demand more. I did. I got it. It was a new world for me. It didn't leave the barn—yet—but a seed had been planted.

One day, Celia came to the barn and saw me hugging Chey's lovely head and kissing her. "OK," said Celia, "We need to have a conversation. You need to decide whether you want this to be your pet . . . or your horse."

In all the riding I'd done, the relationship between me and the horse was never examined. That question made me think about all the relationships in my life, and what the difference was between a pet and horse, a friend and an acquaintance, a lover and a companion. I began looking at the world differently.

With a horse, the deal is: I take care of you and you do what I ask. If the horse is not doing what you want it to, you figure out why and try different things, but you have a right to expect a response. Never before in my entire life to this moment, had I ever felt I had a right to anything. Of course, there will be some things that particular horse is never going to be able to do. You have to recognize that, too. The main thing is: Do they try? You always reward the try.

This understanding started seeping into my human world. When I started thinking about people the way I thought about horses, things started getting better. When I started feeling I had a right to expect certain things . . . and that there are certain things certain *people* are never going to be able to do.

Like dealing with Lindsay, the unpleasant boarder. This was the woman who had not hesitated to tell me what I was doing wrong with Shammes or Nifty. She had on one occasion come up to me after a ride on Nifty, shaking a finger inches from my nose, saying, "You are going to ruin this horse just like you did the last one!"

One summer day, she had her horse on the crossties she considered "hers," presumably because they were the crossties closest to her stall. Chey didn't live indoors, so she didn't have a stall. Since there are a limited number of stations to crosstie horses, it is a general courtesy that one doesn't leave a horse who is crosstied in the aisle unless to get or put away tack, or get a grooming tool you might not have handy. If one person has a horse and needs to pass a horse in the aisle, the convention is that they say, "Excuse me, _____, may I pass?" to which the reply is, "Certainly!" and the owner of the tied horse releases one of the crossties, moves the horse over, and stands next to it while the first person/horse passes. Then they reclip the horse to the released crosstie and continue what they were doing.

I had just finished a lesson on Chey and wanted to hose her off because she was hot and sweaty. I came into the barn at the "ring" side, and clipped Chey at a station to the rear of Lindsay's horse. By now, Chey would stand, nervously, on crossties. The shower stall where we bathed horses was next to Lindsay's horse's nose. Lindsay was having a conversation with someone sitting just outside the barn entrance on the other side of the shower stall. I asked Lindsay, "Excuse me, can I pass?" To which the answer was, "No, I'm busy, go around!" That would mean: Exit the barn by the far entrance, walk around the outside of the barn to enter at the near entrance, and go into the shower stall that was right in front of Lindsay's horse. A spurt of anger popped into me at all the flaws of Lindsay that statement revealed, but I went around. I yielded as I always did. I had no resources with which to address thoughtless or aggressive people.

But the lessons I learned from Chey were finding a home in me. I must say that Chey was a quicker learner than me, because it only took Chey a couple of tries to figure stuff out, and it took me months. But I began to change.

The day came when I was grooming Chey on the crossties. We were on "Lindsay's" crossties, because they happened to be closest to the tack room that had my saddle in it. My western saddle weighs about forty-five pounds. That is about 40 percent of what *I* weigh, so carrying it any distance down the aisle is something I try to avoid. The other four crosstie stations in the barn were free.

Lindsay came into the barn, leading her horse. "Move your horse back one. I want to use those crossties," she said. This time I didn't fume. Or move. I just said, "No, we're good here," and went on brushing Chey. Lindsay exploded, calling me rude and thoughtless and I don't know what else. I had to chuckle to myself. It may have been the first time in my life I stood my ground with a human. I learned it from Chey.

So, I tried to give myself over to this horse, and my lessons, and tried to stop trying.

It was now April 2009.

I'd been very, very tired for several months, and that also led to depression. A routine visit to the eye doctor revealed I had developed glaucoma. I started taking medication for that. Getting older, I guess.

Such wonderful things with Chey. Celia rode her again and was amazed at how much stronger she was than when she first came. She still didn't like her much, but acknowledged the horse was capable of more than she initially thought. Warmed my heart, to hear that, since it means I have been working her appropriately and well. And then something happened that showed me how her mind has come toward me, too.

There were a couple of women at the barn my age or so, who each had a horse they loved and rode, but none of them felt comfortable riding their horses outside of the ring. They were nice women, and I think I was the one who came up with the idea of doing a "drill team." We would practice formation riding in the ring. I had in mind to eventually do it to music, maybe even with "uniforms" (like a plume taped to our helmets!). Because all of our horses were chestnuts, we called ourselves the Chestnut Confederation, or, occasionally, the Ridgehollow Ladies' Light Horse. We did real simple stuff, but the great thing about riding in formation is it makes you be specific and precise. The more precise you can be on horseback, the better you ride. It makes you and your horse quicker and lighter. We would plan on riding together every Thursday. We would make up routines or bring them from manuals of drills and dressage moves.

That day, I was in the ring with the Chestnut Confederation, and we were playing at our dressage exercises. I had already discovered Chey was the kind of horse who would allow you to take off your jacket while in the saddle, or put it on, and she wouldn't freak out. I had also seen I could trot over to the fence and lay my jacket on it without incident. Sally had brought a sheaf of papers she got from a dressage manual that showed various mounted exercises. She didn't need to hold it while we were riding, and I offered to take it, and ride over to the fence to rest it on a fencepost while we rode since Chey is so good at that sort of thing. However horses are funny, and you can never tell but that something completely ordinary to us, like a sheaf of papers, can scare the bejesus out of them. Something about this rippling sheaf scared her to death and she bolted. I dropped the sheaf with Chey in midair, and when she had calmed down enough that I could safely dismount, I got off and went to her head, meaning to work on "despooking" her (that is, gradually desensitizing her to the item that scares her). She looked at me and I saw in her enormous eyes not only fear, but a visible, *Help me! Save me!*

How could I fail to be both touched and proud, that we had

gotten to a point where my horse actually looks to me to save her. I never thought I'd earn that trust. I didn't know how it could be. I embraced her head and told her silently that she was OK. Then I went about despooking her.

As we worked together, I came to know some feelings I could not remember ever having felt before. I, who had always felt insignificant and impotent, felt what it was like to be trusted by someone bigger and stronger than me. I, who had spent most of my life praying I wouldn't be hurt, felt what it was like to be looked to for protection. And I felt something just wonderful. After the nine weeks I had spent in training with Carl and Terry, I felt the supreme joy of knowing what I could do to help some-one I love be not afraid.

Our First Trip Off the Farm

Among the many wonderful things you can do with horses is something called a hunter pace, or, simply, a pace. This is basically an organized trail ride with divisions, fast, slow, and western (for the type of saddle). People in the western division presumably will not be taking the jumps. It is possible to jump in a western saddle, but it requires some finesse to avoid disemboweling yourself on the saddle horn.

My first pace was in Lewisboro, New York, on October 4, 2009. People from my barn were going, and there was room in a horse trailer for us.

Chey loaded but was so frightened to be in the trailer, I felt I had failed her. I had hoped—after the work in the spring at Carl and Terry's—that she would be OK, but she was drenched with sweat when I took her out after the forty-minute ride. She was anxious and showing it by dancing around, head high, body tense, searching for her buddies, but she let me saddle and bridle

Going up . . .

. . . and coming down!

her. And once I got on her and started asking her to do figure eights and circles, she seemed a little less concerned. She performed wonderfully at the pace. We even took a jump!

But I felt I had failed her, because she had been so frightened in the horse trailer.

When I went to see her the next day, she was reluctant, although obedient. I noticed it and decided that it should be a day for rebuilding the relationship. I tried to reassure her, let her graze, and then groomed her. For the first time, as I rubbed the soft curry over her trapezoid, she turned around to groom me. Oh, what a wonderful moment: I had found a good place and was doing it right, so it made her feel good. She turned to me in kindness and appreciation to return the favor. It was the first time she treated me like another horse. What an honor!

Then, I had to worm her. This usually involves placing a large syringe full of worming product into the horse's mouth and shooting it in for the horse to swallow. "Good luck," the barn staff said, shaking their heads as they went on to other duties. Chey was frightened again, tossing her head over and over. But then I did something. I put the wormer down, took a moment to talk to her quietly, and ran my finger over her lips. Then I put my finger gently in the corner of her mouth, and when she opened it, I took my finger away and said, "That's all it is . . . you're a good girl, that's all it is." I did that one more time. Then I took up the wormer and gave it to her. After she took it all in, she dropped her head into me for reassurance, which I was delighted to give her. "What a good girl you are . . . what a wonderful horse," petting her lovely head and hugging her. Then we went out and had some grass.

I realized that when Chey is frightened, I need to move away and take her back to where she is more comfortable. This horse will do it for me: At certain times, she just needs more of my support. I will never let her face an obstacle without it again.

Perhaps, the next time I am frightened, I will remember what worked for Chey and try it on myself.

And I did have occasion to be frightened again. Because I expected to be traveling to other events, I felt we needed to spend some time getting Chey comfortable with the horse trailer. It was not working. As I mentioned, when horses get frightened, you are quickly reminded of how incredibly strong they are, and how quickly things can go wrong. And as Sancho Panza says in *Man of La Mancha*, "whether the stone hits the pitcher, or the pitcher hits the stone, it's going to be bad for the pitcher."

Almost everyone who passed us felt they knew what I should do, and told me, loudly and repeatedly. One friend kept insisting I get her trainer to help me. "Get Patty," she'd insist over and over. "Patty is wonderful. Patty can do it in a minute. Patty will make her *love* going into the trailer. Get Patty. PATTY! GET PATTY!" I wanted to scream, *I need to do it myself!*

By this time, I had completed my nine-week training program. I had had Chey for the last module, and she took it with me. One of the things we had worked in that module was trailer loading. By the conclusion of that session, I had loaded Chey and several other horses dozens of times into every kind of trailer there was: step-up, slant-load, stock trailer, ramp load. Chey had loaded beautifully in the program, she knew how to load, and *I* was the one who needed to make it work. I wanted to be a horse trainer, so it was a huge blow to my pride. But more importantly, Lily's trainer is not going to be there when I want to go somewhere, or when I want to come back. Of course, a professional can get the horse to load, but it is more than loading the horse. It is more than teaching the horse to load. It is about having a relationship with the horse. It is about being a leader who has earned the horse's trust. This is what I needed to learn. This was proving to be harder than I thought. I was getting depressed.

It was autumn, and I found a day to go into the city to manage a quick visit with my old friend Jeff over coffee. I was talking about the bout of self-doubt I had just gone through, and how, since situationally I had everything I ever wanted—a horse—the only thing left was fundamental issues with me. The self-esteem issue continued to plague me, though I have had a life in the theater, on Wall Street, I had the rich and wild fifteen summers I spent cowboying in Wyoming; I'd made a fortune, which was barely sufficient to warrant the name but was permitting me to pursue my lifelong dream. I had found the right horse, had good equipment, and had the time to see her almost every day. But all this was not enough. I should have done better. And I wished I were better.

Jeff is such a good friend, always supportive, always positive. He helps me see things more clearly. He can analyze the dynamics of a situation, which is one of the talents that have contributed to his substantial success in finance. He asked, "What, exactly, do you want to be able to do and can't yet?" He made me actually think about it, and the answer was that I wanted to be able to deal with aggressive, resistant horses. And then I realized, I am not very good at dealing with aggressive people, either. I am almost never sure I'm right . . . but that is not something situational, it something central to my entire life so far, implanted by the upbringing I'd had, and that was the central issue I still had to address. I still had problems living in myself, although I loved my animals and my time with them, and enjoyed my friends in the country. I had been working at this so long (namely, the self-esteem issue that was at the core of all the negativity in my life), and it seemed I'd come so little distance, I just wish I knew what I had to do to get there.

Reassessing

It was winter 2009–2010. I'd been very sick for about six weeks, the flu and its antecedent and successive misery. My friends at the barn convinced me to go to the doctor. Turns out I am hypothyroid, which runs through my family. Smoking, or rather nicotine, provides a bit of a bounce to my energy and mental acuity, but of course, it is not helpful to my overall health. I started synthetic thyroid hormone medicine.

When I hooked up again with Celia, I had said I wanted to go as high as I could, which generally means competition. Celia said that if competition is my goal, Chey was not the horse. "If you want to load into a trailer, go somewhere, get out, and compete to win, this is not the horse for you. She'll never get there. This horse is a piece of shit, and you need to get yourself a 'good' horse."

What? You mean: Sell Chey?! I couldn't. It would be like selling a member of my family. I had enough money to live with J as a roommate but not enough to support a string of horses. It was time to reexamine what I wanted. Did I want to compete? Or did I want a long-term relationship with a horse? Was it OK to want the latter more than the former? Not in Celia's eyes. I was torn.

I found that as I progressed through my life with horses, I realized things about other aspects of my life. Dealing with horses requires a presence and an attention that led me to some interesting places. For example, I realized that J had some justification for feeling that as I was up here all the time, I had a greater responsibility for upkeep. I also recognized that when I vacuumed and cleaned the kitchen and bathroom, and did all the laundry before he arrived, he wouldn't notice. So I just made it a point to do all that, which I was doing anyway, while he was here so he could see I was doing it. It was a reasonable hypothesis; but, nothing changed. Instead of beating myself up about it, I treated it like a lesson with Chey. OK, that didn't work. Try something else.

His complaint with me was that I didn't do enough work around the place. At some point, I thought I had an answer. "Why don't we make a list?" I said. "Make a list, so I know what it is you expect of me, so I know what I have to do. And that way, I'll also know what responsibilities you are comfortable with, and all the chores will get done, and everyone will do their share, and no one will have any reason to be angry at the other!" He said nothing and walked away. We never made a list. We still went food shopping together, but now, we each bought out own stuff and started labeling it. The refrigerator developed boundaries: "his" side and mine.

But we still went places together and traded Christmas/Hannukah and birthday presents. About that time, I found what I thought would be a wonderful Christmas gift. It was a silver pocket watch, engraved by Montana Silversmiths. I thought it was the most beautiful object I'd ever seen, and it would show how much I was still committed to him despite our growing friction. That Christmas Day, I handed him his gift, and he handed me mine. He opened his. "Hanh!" he said. Now, what was that supposed to mean? I wondered. "Open yours," he said. I did. It was a silver pocket watch, with the Saint-Gaudens Walking Liberty silver half dollar on the face. My gift to him paled in comparison to this piece of actual history. I loved it.

But back to Celia. When she pointed out that Chey was not the horse to take me to the next level, it hurt. I felt I owed so much to Chey. I had taken her life as my responsibility, and I could not conceive of abdicating that role. Celia and her husband bought and sold horses all the time, looking for good horses who could take her to the next level, keeping the ones who worked, selling the ones who didn't. I asked, "Aren't you concerned about what happens to the horses after you sell them?" "No," they answered. "Why should we be? Not our problem, then." Having spent Wednesday afternoons at the horse rescue for the last three years, and having seen what sometimes happens to horses people didn't want anymore, I was taken aback. But they were certainly pros. Was this the way to think about horses?

Do I want to have a horse, or do I want to be a horsewoman? Does it have to be one or the other? It's a hard choice right now. Over all, I was so much happier than I had ever been, now that I was improving with my gentle horse, and not getting hurt. Everyone noticed. Lucero, a friend, said it was because I was in love—that was why the world was right. She was right. I was in love. With Chey. But . . . Celia wanted me to get another horse. Her horse-trading husband could find me one. Celia would work with me until I could handle it.

I didn't have to make that choice immediately. The most

important choices I've made, the ones that have paid off so well, were scary, but in a way, easy. I knew when it was time to leave theater and go back to school to learn a trade, and when it became time to leave finance and follow my heart's deepest longing. I will never abandon Chey, but I can conceive of a time when I will be ready for another horse. I don't know how it will happen yet, or when. But I can see it may come.

Winter Wisdom

I had another insight. It'd been some serious winter with riding limited by footing and a frozen ring. I missed days because of weather. So I was thinking more about temperature management and warming up and down. I was careful about warming Chey up, but one day I understood how I could do it better and more efficiently.

I was looking for guidance on how long I should walk, how many minutes, then how many minutes to trot, etc., but I was using the wrong side of my brain, the analytical side. I realized, I would never find the answer in print. I had to feel it in Chey. When I let my mind go and focused my senses on her, it became easier to read her body. I'm sure I've had this sensation before, but one day I had one of those moments of understanding. We all want to become one with our horse. That winter, I saw in a deeper way what that can mean: It is the balance of two bodies in motion. I've often called it like dancing. It is. With a thousand-pound partner.

How could I give up this horse now! So, I guess I'd made that choice, at least, for the moment. Sometimes you discover that what you want is not always what you thought you'd want. It is a mistake to cling to old paradigms, merely because they are comfortable. I'm finding that once I let go of preconceptions, and experience the moment, I am making better choices about my life. And I was so very contented. What a wonderful time I was having.

Life with Chey was good. We continued to learn about each other. She was calmer; I was more confident. I was learning the difference between being positive in my approach and being negative. Those ugly knuckles relaxed their grip on my mind. And I realized: I hadn't taken a Xanax in months. I didn't even know if I still had any.

I was taking a lesson with Celia, and it was midwinter, lots of ice in the ring. In the winter, I'd put snowshoes on Chey, shoes with pads to keep the snow out of her hooves and borium studs to grab on the ice so she'd have better traction. However, that day, despite the studs, Chey slipped on the ice, lost her balance, and plummeted, stumbling, unable to catch her balance, toward a somersault with me on her back, right into the fence. I, seeing that there was absolutely nothing I could do but stay out of her way, sat back, completely relaxed, loose legs, soft rein, and let her find her balance again, which she did. "You handled that perfectly!" Celia said. "But that one gave me a few more gray hairs."

Beginning to Notice Things

I was studying my horse, and the other horses I was exposed to, all the time. I still couldn't read them as well as I'd hoped: What they're thinking? Why they're doing or not doing whatever? But oddly, I found I was getting much better at seeing things about people. I began to notice things about people whose favor I once sought. When they'd talk about getting out of jury duty, or how the cop was lying about that second DWI, or how smart those Chinese people are, now I didn't just wipe that off the board. I realized that I felt differently about things than they did and maybe I didn't need their acceptance as much as I thought. This was especially the case with my housemate/boyfriend. Things I used to overlook as humorous quirks began to appear very differently to me: his agreeing to anything I say and then ignoring it, his need for ear protection in the form of big padded headphones whenever we were together, his decision that the job was over whenever he chose to walk away from it.

Meanwhile, I so enjoyed being around this horse. Her paddock had a view of the road I drove up to the barn every day. I'd park by the barn and come back down to get her. Chey was always waiting at the gate. Was it possible she recognized my car? I'd bet she did. My ideas about what horses can perceive and understand were changing. Everything I knew before was from books, because that was all I had. Now, I have wonderful Chey, in the flesh, and my education is transformed.

We just trotted some circles, worked on our haunches in, a little lope, because we had done a long trail ride the day before. She was lovely, except for a poor side pass to the left, but we had gotten two good steps in at last. I really enjoyed being around this horse.

One day, I knew they were planning to do some work on the drainage on Chey's side of the facility, so those horses would be, temporarily, in different paddocks. I also knew there was a new horse coming at any time. As I drove up to the barn, I thought the horse in Chief's old paddock was the newcomer. My breath caught at the sight of the dazzling, muscular bronze horse, wind rippling a mane and tail the color of sugar, lifting her head, perking her ears to look at my car. *What a beautiful horse,* I thought. Then I recognized her. The horse was Chey.

However, the better things went with the horse, the worse they got with J. When we bought the house together, I'd made it a condition that one day, someday, I'd have a horse. Perhaps that was one of the occasions when he agreed and then ignored me; or perhaps he thought having a horse was like having a boat, you tie it to a mooring and go out on it every now and then. It wasn't great when we only spent weekends at the house and I was riding other people's horses. It was much worse, now that I was living there full-time. I started having bad dreams again: losing my horse, losing my cat, driving off the road, cell phone dead. I'd wake up with my stomach in knots and my heart racing. I needed a kind word from him and would make breakfast or wash the floor or do anything to get it. Familiar behavior, familiar response. Not good enough. His scowl became semi-permanent. Why didn't I leave? I was just too frightened to be alone.

I rode with a woman who had an old Thoroughbred originally from the track. He was a kind old horse, and she said I could ride him anytime she couldn't. She rode him hunt seat (i.e., English) while I rode Chey western. I was feeling pretty good about things, and asked Celia to give me a lesson in hunt seat, on Theo. Actually, until now, I had mostly ridden English since that's what was available in the city, and was the style in Ireland and Morocco, where I had ridden on vacations. Celia asked, "Are you sure?" "Yeah!" I said. "I got this."

I had opened up a can of whoop ass. I was totally abashed. I thought I rode better than that, but my legs were swinging all over, I couldn't find the center and I almost fell off Theo twice. Hanging on his neck with my legs both on his left side. Toward the end of the second hour, I just couldn't hold it anymore, and we quit. I was certain I'd be able to ride him better than his owner, who unlike me, couldn't ride every day. Celia reminded me that his owner had been riding him for fourteen years. And I was due for a comeuppance. Any time you start to feel too confident around horses, you are due. At least, this time, it was only my pride that was hurt. Celia's influence at that time was so positive, she helped me counteract decades of negative thinking, and I took it as it should be taken: mere data, just information, that's all. For the future.

But the bad dreams still came: I'd be driving somewhere, I'd lose my way, the streets would get narrower and narrower, closing in, my Jeep would turn into a kind of rolling chair that started falling apart, and I'd to hold it together with my hands but I didn't have enough hands. Then I'd have to take the elevator and it would only hold one person and it would be occupied. What was it in my mind that wouldn't let me go? I swear, it would be so cruel and really might kill me, if the day comes that I can't be around horses. But the summer passed, the autumn came, I rode Chey, and we got better and better together every day.

Then a terrible loss: My beloved Goody died on September 5, 2010. I probably should have sent her on sooner, but I couldn't. I couldn't handle the idea of not having Goody to come home to, that warm, purring source of endless, unmitigated love. I couldn't even write about it.

About a month later, Odin came into my life, an older cat, FIV-positive. Of course, he was not Goody, but he was a friendly, level cat who had been around, and was unfailingly appreciative of being given the chance to end his life in a home, instead of in a cage. Goody gave so much love in her life with me, I had enough to spare to foster this elderly, compromised tom and make him as comfortable as I could, for as long as he stayed.

2011: My *Anno Mirabilis*

I was now in my late fifties. I had begun to accept some of the inevitable. My skin was beginning to sag. The wrinkles were popping up weekly. I was on medication for glaucoma and thyroid disease. I was getting heavier, despite going for a cigarette before a snack. In fact, in the fall, I bit the bullet, and gave away all the size sevens and nines, and invested in an assortment of size eleven and twelve jeans and khakis.

It had become winter—and it was time to break out the chaps, the Mountain Horse boots, the severe cold weather riding gear. I have a beautiful pair of chaps—chinks, actually, which is the honest-to-Betsy name for chaps that on an adult would fall about halfway down the leg. Cowboys like them, because in the real world, cowboys are always mounting and dismounting, to open gates, to fix a fence, to doctor a cow. The little chaps make it lots easier to get your leg up to the stirrup, without that tight leather grabbing you from hip to ankle. On me, the chinks came all the way down to my ankles. They had beautiful dark leather overlays, Texas stars, and fringe. It was a wild extravagance I had indulged in during the money years. I was thrilled my life had come to a place where I actually needed to use them.

I brought them out and began to strap them on. They were too tight, even on the last hole. *No!* I cried in my mind. *Enough! I am not going to let these go!*

I needed to lose weight. Seriously. I began to research weight loss diets—not fads, but the best science I could find on the sub-ject, and came up with the Atkins diet. I got the book, read it cover to cover, got a little notebook to monitor my eating and plan my meals, bookmarked the pages with the carb values for everything, and went for it. It. Was. Phenomenal. It takes time to prepare and record your food, and all that water is a pain when you're wearing three layers of clothing, but it worked like you wouldn't believe. I lost two pounds the first week, and a pound a week after that, until I had lost twenty-two pounds. I went from my high of almost 140 pounds to about 118 over a period of about five months. Everything in my closet was loose. I could wear the suit I wore to my first banking interview! And pursuing this diet had other completely unexpected benefits. My eating was one of the things over which I felt I did not always have control. However, the structure of this diet—the three meals and two snacks, the water, and the fact that you are never hungry—those wild cravings, the desperate *need* for a box of Ring Dings, went away. I would still get them, but progress was so visible, and I felt so much energy and so good about myself when I ate this way, I was able to hold on. Even after I tapered back to "normal" eating, it was a new normal. I had been re-educated about por-tions, ate virtually no processed food, and my new normal was the healthiest approach to food I had ever had.

Then, at a routine glaucoma check with my ophthalmologist, we made a stunning discovery. At the relatively young age of fifty-eight, I had developed cataracts. He was as surprised as I was. But there was nothing for it. They had to be removed. Living in a house in the country, not being able to drive is a serious problem, and I wouldn't be able to if I didn't take care of this.

Then there's the procedure. I discovered that these days, they don't just remove the cataract. They remove the lens of your eye and replace it with a synthetic lens. *Gaak.* But the good thing is, they can replace it with a lens corrected for your vision. I had been wearing glasses since I was four. They could give me lenses that would give me 20/20 vision. And correct for the astigmatism I had developed. Wow. One drawback, the synthetic lenses can not flex like natural lenses, so I would need reading glasses, but so do most people after forty, when natural lenses also begin to lose their flexibility. With contact lenses, we explored giving me one eye with reading vision and one eye with distance vision, but I was not one of the people who can adapt to that, so I opted for 20/20, and the surgery was scheduled for March 2011. I arranged with my old friend Fred to pick me up after the surgery and take me home, which, at the time, meant my Manhattan apartment, which I was still renting. Turns out it was fortunate I still had the apartment, because it would not have been a good idea to travel the two hours back up north after such delicate surgery.

Then I realized something else. If I was still smoking by the time of the surgery, I wouldn't heal as quickly or as thoroughly as if I wasn't. Oh no. Not that. I had been smoking for thirty years; it was one of the obsessive activities that helped me calm my manic mind, gave me a moment's peace and comfort, and I wasn't at all sure I could live without it.

But . . . my eyes. I felt I had to do this. I stopped smoking on January 26, 2011. Remarkably, I found that being on the diet was what saved me. It turned out that I spent the time I would have had a smoke planning, preparing, or noting down what I'd eaten and calculating its values in my daily food chart. I would never have believed it, but I quit. I've cheated once since then, when I was with a smoking crowd and I had too much to drink, but never since. I quit. I am the only person I know who lost weight when they quit smoking.

And I learned something else, as well. I had been a substance abuser my whole life, beginning before my teens, and I was desperately ashamed of it. For all the years I had tried to punish myself into better behavior, it turns out, you can not defeat an addiction, you can not crush the evil, negative, destructive impulses, because stress just makes them stronger, and the harder you fight them, the stronger they get. But you can replace them, squeeze them out to starve, but putting something positive in their place. Good can't come from bad. You have to get it good, first. And funny, the first place I ever heard that was in a Buck Brannaman clinic. He was talking about horses. So much of what worked with horses seemed to be working for me.

By the end of 2011; I was twenty pounds lighter, I had quit smoking, and I had slightly better than 20/20 vision. Wow. That was a good year.

Summer

At Celia's place, I ran into Cordy, that cowgirl who had advised me against buying Chey. You sure don't have to worry about holding up your end of the conversation when she's around. Not only has she done everything, she's done it bigger, badder, rougher, and tougher than you. When I was in Wyoming, the boss would haul along a sheep wagon to sleep in on the cattle drives, a most ingenious little cowboy trailer that looks like an eight-foot Quonset hut on wheels, with a wood stove and an incredible variety of shelves and counters that can be rearranged to make sleeping quarters for three or a dining table or any-thing else you can think of. Cordy's spent some time out there, so I asked her if she's ever seen one. "Ho, no, we didn't have such luxuries, nope, we had to sleep on the sagebrush or in the saddle. . . ." Yeah, yeah, I just asked if you'd ever seen one. Then she jumped on that bandwagon about Chey: "You gotta dump that piece of shit horse and get a good one." She sees horses as tools, as a business, as a way to get belt buckles. I see them as something else. Right or wrong, Chey was not a business to me, or a machine, or a tool. She was and is a relationship to me, one I enjoy, a horse who is happy to see me, a participant in whatever I say. Perhaps I wanted too little, but I was so happy to have a horse who didn't hurt me, that I could ride any time I wanted whether or not she'd worked the day before or even the week before. Some horses have to be lunged for twenty minutes before you can get on.

On the home front, J was pretty good. He wanted to redo the bathroom. I wanted a lawn tractor adequate to our property. I said I'd go in on the bathroom if he'd go in on the tractor. He said he'd think about it.

I had another lesson with Celia. The lessons had changed, they were becoming less fun, more pounding. I was so tired of hearing "connect with the horse, you're riding defensively, feel the hind legs." I was just not feeling these things, and I was getting ferociously frustrated. "Fix that! Fix that!" Fix *what*? "Can't you feel that?" Feel *what*? There were days I got off after a lesson so discouraged I didn't even want to ride the next day. Still not smoking (and it pissed me off that Celia just took it for granted that I was not!). Bought a small cake. Ate half of it.

I was bored with my diet, bored with my lessons, bored with the gym. I was bored of everything except Chey. She was waiting at her gate when I came to get her. She followed me quietly up to the barn, stood peacefully while I groomed her and tacked her up, did the leg yields and side passes and everything else I had been trying to do with her, getting lighter and lighter all the time. I felt like we were dancing.

It was time for her EquiSpot treatment, like a tick treatment for horses, a little tube you squeeze between the ears, along the spine, and up the back of each leg. Maybe it stings a little, it's got permethrin. She doesn't like it and usually bounces around when

I try to apply it, making it difficult to put on properly. This time, I showed it to her. Her head lifted in alarm. "Look," I said, "here it is. I know you don't like this. But it keeps the bugs away and I hope you will let me put it on you." And she did. She stood like a statue. I loved this horse. This was what Deb and everyone else was talking about. This was how it was supposed to be.

I was wondering if I should buy J out. He suggested it twice. He should be OK with it.

I was taking dressage lessons with two of my barn mates with Livia Barrow, who was quite a contender in competitive dressage in her time. I was thrilled to discover that the patterns were easy for me and Chey. Precision and accuracy were something we worked on every day, so when I asked for it with other horses in the ring, on command, Chey was there for me. Maybe she didn't have the snap and style a better built horse might, or a better-trained horse might, but we met our marks and got our transitions as well or better than the other people I was riding with, and I was proud of her.

I listened to an interview with a human psychotherapist who specializes in using horses to reach the human psyche, and Jane Savoie, a world-renowned dressage master. They talked about how horses respond to you when you are authentic, and how we can't be "authentic" all the time. It would be like having no skin, but horses can sense when you're not all there. And how emotional issues will show up in your riding and in your relationship with your horse. *Hmmm.*

I called Dr. Amery who had tried so hard with Shammes, to come do some work on Chey. When I saw his report, I was aghast. Virtually every joint in her body except her fetlocks was compromised. Later, he told me that her condition was not exceptional for a horse her approximate age (we didn't know her actual age) who had never had any bodywork (and undoubtedly, never been worked by someone who really knew how to understand and help a horse through biomechanical limitations), so I felt a little better. I did arrive at a new understanding of what Celia has been talking about when she says her movement is not good. Her movement can't be good when her anatomy limits the range of motion through a number of her joints. However, after Dr. Amery's first visit, Chey not only picked up her left lead, which had always been difficult for her; she offered it! I was elated. A few more visits, some supplements, more care in warming up and cooling down.

I rode with Kay, Theo's human, on the trail after the chiropractic adjustment, cautioning her that we needed to go easy, no sudden moves or quick starts or stops. She agreed. And then halfway through the ride, there was a steep hill in the woods, and she let her horse bolt at a dead gallop up it, forcing me to either follow or have a major battle with my horse in a confined space. I felt the battle might be more traumatic, and let her go. "I thought we agreed nothing sudden!" I yelled at my "friend." "Oh, I just couldn't help it, it looked like so much fun!" she giggled. Having just spent $450 on a chiropractic session with my horse, which the violent and abrupt movement may have undone, I didn't find it that entertaining.

A Big Step

There was so much going on beyond the barn. Paces, horse shows, trail rides. Real stuff. It sounded so exciting, and, despite Chey's discomfort in a horse trailer, I had some opportunities to ride in other people's horse trailers to some events. I began to think . . . maybe I should have my own. Getting a horse trailer is not that difficult, but having a vehicle to pull one (or stop one, with a ton of horse in it) is a different story. And I had been pretty free with money up to now, but that couldn't continue if I wanted to keep doing this. The mistakes with the first two horses had been expensive. I had had cataract surgery and some expensive dental work since I retired. My resources had been depleted. And there was a chance I was going to be living alone. Needed to think about this.

I was trying to be honest. I liked him. I just didn't like living with him. And the feeling was mutual. So I started rehearsing some lines. "I'd like my own space." Not clear enough. "You don't want to live with me" will make him defensive. "I don't want to live with you" ditto. But I thought I found one that would work: "We liked each other better before we started sharing a house. Let's go back there." If I gave up the apartment, I might be able to do it. I spoke to all the people I know who cared about me, and they agreed this might be the way. Win-win. Positive. No accusations or disapproval. He seemed good today. Maybe if we took a hike . . .

Keep positive. Win-win.

But . . . back to the horse trailer. A lot of people pull horse trailers with SUVs; some eight-cylinder SUVs have enough horsepower, but I came to learn that it's more than that. You need a robust transmission for pulling, powerful brakes, a long wheelbase to counteract sway. I wanted a factory-installed tow package; a mechanic can put one in, but I decided I wanted a vehicle that from the time it was sheet steel, had been designed to pull. Then my farrier, who had helped me so much with Chey, offered some advice: "Get a pickup truck. If you are going to have a life with horses, you are going to need to schlep hay, tack trunks, buckets; you don't want to have to throw a couple of bales of hay in the back of your Jeep."

I began researching vehicles, horsepower, torque, gear ratios, differentials. I needed something bigger than a Ranger, but I expected to only be pulling a two-horse trailer, and the bigger you go, the worse the gas mileage. I decided something like the Ford F150 or the GM1500 would do it. I wanted a crew cab, because it would also be my "car," and it occurred to me that it would be really unpleasant to have to load groceries in an open truck bed in a pouring rain, or in the snow. I would look for something used, low mileage.

I had a mechanic I trusted in the town. I found him after an unsatisfactory experience with another one, who needed three tries to fix my ignition when it was off, and started with the most-expensive option first. This mechanic always started with the least-expensive option, checked out things in general when he had the car on the lift, and could be counted on in a jam. I spoke to him about what I wanted. He got online right then and started searching. I was a little unprepared to move quite so quickly, but within days, he found a vehicle at a dealer's auction he thought might be suitable. "Can I see it?" I asked. "No!" he said. "You're not a dealer!" but I saw it on the computer screen, and he went out there and checked it out and it seemed right and the price was reasonable (and worked out, oddly, to about a dollar per mile on the odometer, twenty-six thousand dollars) and he went over it in detail and the engine was good and the structure was good (although it might need front ball joints pretty soon). It was happening so fast and I wasn't really sure I was ready, but I told him "OK!" I got the money out of my

Ain't it a beauty?

investment accounts, I drove out there with him to pick it up, and the first time I saw it, or ever drove a pickup truck, was when I drove my truck back home. He took my old Jeep in payment of his fee.

OMG, I had done it! I had bought a truck! This was October 2011. I remember, because I was barely used to driving it, when we got hit with the Great October Snowstorm of 2011.

I couldn't quite believe it. Here, I was a New Yorker who never even had a car until I bought the house upstate; and I was driving a pickup truck! It looked so big at first, and it was so powerful, but it was very gentle and cooperative, and had lots of ways to make towing safer. I was sure we would get to know each other well, and that this truck would take me places at least as pleasant and happy as those to which my beloved Jeep had always driven me.

October 2011

It was right about this time that Steve Jobs died. It was a so‑
cietally defining event, for those of my generation, who entered
society at the same time computers did. As I heard him speak
though the remembrances, I got the impression that Steve Jobs
lived his life as if he knew it would be short. I heard him say:
Your time is limited, so don't waste it living someone else's life.
Don't be trapped by dogma—which is living with the results of
other people's thinking. Don't let the noise of other's opinions
drown out your own inner voice. And most important: Have
the courage to follow your heart and intuition. He could have
been speaking from the past directly to me, at this time in my
life. He also said that every day, he would ask himself, "If this
was the last day of your life, would you spend it the way you're
planning to today?" And if the answer was "No" too many days
in a row, he knew something had to change.

If tomorrow were to be the last day of my life, I would want
to spend it as I do every day now, with Chey for a few hours. I
took the leap and bought the equipment. My rig would take us
both farther than we could have imagined, just as this life has
taken me places I hadn't anticipated. I had reached a stage of life
where I could say, with reason, "What was I waiting for?" I had
come to the understanding that I didn't know how long I'd have
to do this, how long I would be able to ride and drive, and it
was finally Jam Today.

I started researching horse trailers, getting depressed at the
prices for new ones. They could cost more than my truck, and
while I had some money, spending it in these amounts was
breathtaking; after all, this money would have to last me the rest
of my life. But a few weeks later, I found a horse trailer, used, a
cute white Kingston with red trim.

It was, in fact, owned by the woman from whom I'd bought
Chey.

The horse trailer

It didn't seem expensive—three thousand dollars—and, what felt like on impulse, I bought it. The lady dropped it off at Suzie's, who hitched me up, and gave me some good advice: "Treat every light as if it will turn red. Drive like you're balancing a wineglass on the dashboard. You can do this! You can do this!" I was barely comfortable driving the truck, and there I was, pulling my horse trailer, making a *left* on to Route 22 to take it home. I held my breath for twenty-four minutes.

Wow. I had a truck and a horse trailer. Welcome to Chapter Two.

Not So Fast

Yeah, so, now I had a truck and horse trailer. I was terrified of each, individually, and both, collectively. I started driving on high alert, jumping at every creak and bounce, everything was new to me. I drove it to a trailer place where they checked it out, brakes, body, electrics. My heart would race as I would pull it into a yard, or, especially, out into traffic. Then the day came when I drove it to the barn.

I don't know about other trailers, but a horse trailer is designed with about three fail-safes; if the hitch fails, there are chains. If the chains fail, there is a guy wire that trips and sets the trailer brakes. The guy wire is just that, a wire clipped to the frame of the pulling vehicle. If it gets stretched beyond a certain point, it trips.

The first time I drove it to the barn, I was tense as a drum, my eyes and ears straining in every direction, thinking about the length of the truck plus the length of the trailer, the increased mass, and it occurred to me that, once loaded, I will be an eight-ton unit rolling along the highway at fifty-five miles per hour. You have to be very respectful of inertia when you are part of something like that.

So, I drove as slowly as I could, making the turns, holding my breath, looking in all mirrors simultaneously, knuckles clenched. The last turn was a very sharp right. And as I dragged the trailer alongside the ring, one of the boarders started yelling, "Your wheels are locked! Stop, Stop! Your wheels are locked!" She came running up in a panic, which set me off seven alarms. Oh my God, what'd I do? What's wrong? I jumped out of the truck and looked at the hitch, not knowing what to do. OMG.

Marco, who had helped me out so much with the earlier horses strolled over. "Don' worry," he said. "I's nothin'. When you make the turn, you pull the trip wire. I's just set a little too tight. Everythin' is OK, is working like i' should." Oh. Thank. God. He plugged it back in, reset the brake, and the wheels were turning again. I aged a year in a minute and drove the trailer home where I faced the challenge of parking it in my backyard. My house was on a hill, with a longish driveway and a leveled parking area right behind. After that, the three acres dropped down in a meaningful slope to the pond. As it happened, I had just exactly enough space to park this little horse trailer on the level area behind the house. Not three feet more. In fact, not two feet more.

It took about an hour and a half to back it in properly, but when I did, it was nice and straight and I was proud. I developed routines, mnemonics, to remember how to hitch it up properly: seven outside, two inside. The outside ones were: ball, sleeve, cotter pin, winch, chain, chain, tripwire; the inside ones were tow/haul mode on, and adjust gain on trailer brakes. The more

I did it, the more comfortable I felt. I continually reminded my-self, you don't have to be an Olympic athlete, or a rocket scien-tist, to pull a horse trailer. Just look at some of the people who do. That gave me some comfort.

The Fall of Ridgehollow

The barn felt like a family. I've already mentioned that Debbie, the manager, was the kindest, most positive person I've ever met, with the kind of integrity that really makes you take notice. She had been a NYC mounted police officer before she retired in connection with an injury that precluded her continuing in police work. She's about ten years younger than me. She worked seven days a week. In the seven years she had been managing the place, she had taken only one day off, and that was the day her dog died.

As is typical at horse facilities, she lived on the premises. She cleaned paddocks. She dragged the ring. She cleaned the eight stalls for the indoor horses, and the twenty or so paddocks where the indoor horses were turned out and the "rough board" horses (like Chey) lived full-time. She fed. She hayed. She plowed the snow. She paid the bills. She had invested substantial sums of her own money in the place, trusting in the goodwill of the owner, buying automatic waterers and such. There were helpers from time to time, but at the beginning, it was pretty much Deb and Marco. She was unfailingly kind to me in my quest to be a horsewoman, and undoubtedly saved my life by urging me to sell Nifty. She advised me, when I asked questions or needed help, and showed me how. She arranged birthday cakes for all the boarders, and we had Christmas parties and July 4 barbecues. It was a wonderful place, and the face of it was Debbie.

But then things changed. The owner was an entrepreneurial type, and he had a hand in a bunch of businesses of which this boarding stable was only one. He started behaving erratically. He began drinking, or at least he started showing up drunk. I was there late one afternoon and saw him driving the backhoe precipitously on top of the manure pile, which was nearly a story high, as the light faded. I urged him to let me drive him up to the house. He made a pass, but when I demurred, he let it go. He got a new girlfriend, one of the boarders, a middle-aged woman who had been recently divorced. She had been a businesswoman who had been a housewife for years. I always wondered if she'd ever use her MBA again. It turned out, she would. At Ridgehollow.

The vibe changed. There was tension, there were bills that didn't get paid, and deliveries of hay and grain that were delayed. The horses were never without food, but the delays caused Deb a lot of stress.

Dissention started in the ranks. What had been a big happy family became an acrimonious collection of factions. No one was against Debbie; it was more those who felt angry and betrayed by the owner, and those who liked Debbie but didn't want to get involved. They had a barn that was priced right and near the trails and that was all they cared about as long as the horses were good.

Then, we got the word, the girlfriend was moving in. Then, there was a rumor that the girlfriend's daughter was heard in the tack shop saying she and her mother would be running a horse farm soon. We didn't believe it; Deb had done so much for the place, so much for the boarders, we just didn't believe it could be true. Rumors, you know.

Then, one day, Deb informed us all, with no fanfare or emotion, that she was told her employment at Ridgehollow would terminate on December 15, 2012. She would also have to vacate the property, on which she had been living for the last seven years. She never made a complaint or accusation, although this must have hurt her terribly. You see, the owner was her brother.

"If you're leaving the fifteenth, I'm leaving the fourteenth," I said. I had been to a clinic at a farm about twenty minutes north of my house. The horses there lived in large fields, mares in one, geldings in another, with a few separate paddocks for the elderly or the sick. The price was right, there was a great ring, and we could ride on the property. It was also convenient by trailer to some of the nicest trails in Dutchess County. I contacted the owner, and Chey and I were set to move.

Chey was still not good at trailering. I was still afraid. I called Celia and told her I was going to have to move Chey, and could she help me. Celia was aware of some of the issues. "Do you know what the problem is?" she asked, smiling. "Uh . . . she's afraid?" I said. "She doesn't give to pressure," said Celia. Celia gave me what's called an unbreakable halter. It was woven out of one piece of poly with a short lead line. "Put this on her. Tie her high and short to a big tree, and get out of the way. Do this a few times before we have to trailer her." "I hope this works," I said. "I love this horse, but trailering is going to be a deal breaker." Celia stood back in surprise, pleasure on her face. "My, how you've changed," she said.

I discussed this with Livia, too, the dressage master. "Tie her to a tree, short and high," she said. "At this age (meaning Chey's age), that's the only way to get it done."

I planned to try it the next day. I was pretty scared, and I knew Chey would be able to tell, so I moved as quickly as I could while staying smooth. I didn't want to undertake this where others could see me. Not everyone thought this was a good idea (although the two horse people I respected most did); and this might get a little dicey. I didn't need an audience. Near Chey's paddock there was an oak tree over a foot in diameter. I tied Chey short, her nose almost to the tree, and jumped back. It was well I did. She got her hind legs under her and *heaved* back, giving it everything she had. Her hooves slid forward against the pull. Her head stayed exactly where it was, and the tree held. I began to understand the lesson. Tying her high and short prevented her from getting a leg over the lead line, flipping over backward, or breaking her neck. Pulling back, and not being released, taught her that the jig was up; she could no longer just break away from a tie when she didn't want to be there. That the only way to release pressure was to give in to it. We did this a few more times before the date.

On the day, Celia came, even though she had bronchitis. All my tack and everything were already moved. It was cold, and we were both all bundled up. I'd trailer her. Celia would follow in her vehicle.

"OK," she said. "Let's talk about this. You lead her into the trailer, tie her off fast, and get out of there. Close up the side doors, I'll close up the back, and then get moving. Don't lollygaggle; drive the speed limit. If anything goes wrong in loading her, you just drop the lead line and get your fanny out of here as fast as you can." I took a deep breath. "Maybe we should have a signal or something in case something happens and I need to stop once I'm driving?" I said, querulously. "We are NOT STOP-PING until we get there, I don't care if she turns around and starts climbing out of the trailer!" "OK," I said. I started walking down to get Chey, and then turned to Celia. "You know, I don't want you to do this for me. I want you to show me how, so I don't get hurt." She smiled though her down and gloves. "I know," she said. "I know."

I got Chey, she loaded in, I tied her off, we shut the doors, I got in the truck, put it in tow/haul mode, adjusted brakes, and off we went. I tried to see everything at once, I tried to keep the speed exactly fifty-five miles per hour, anticipating all the lights, over steep hills and sharp turns, watching the road, watching the rear wheels, watching how close the trailer wheels came to the side of the road, watching my alarmed horse through the window of the trailer. We got to the facility, and I turned in. The owner, Louise, a spry woman a few years older than me who had about nine horses and rode most of them daily, was waiting for me with a smile.

"Hi. You can pull in over there," she said, waving at the broad expanse of lawn. "You can back onto that." Holding my breath, I turned the wheel right to move the back of the horse trailer left, and managed to make a pretty straight backup. Celia drove up and parked by the cars, got out, and we did the introductions. "OK," said Celia. "Let's get her out."

She undid the back of the trailer. I was in front holding Chey's lead line. Celia had given me a long one, in case she charged out, so she wouldn't drag me. "You ready?" she called. "Yeah," I said. Celia dropped the butt bar and got out of the way. Chey shifted her weight. "Whoa," I said. She whoa'd. "Back," I said, giving the slightest pressure on the lead line.

Chey backed out carefully and slowly, one step at a time, just like we'd been taught. We cleared the horse trailer. She looked left. She looked right. Then she put her head down to eat grass. Celia smiled at me. "She'll be fine."

We walked Chey over to the paddock in which she would live with her new herd. The paddock was designed with two gates, so horses could be contained in a comfortable area, a bigger area, or released to the whole big field, which was about five acres. Louise had arranged two of the enormous round hay feeders in the comfortable area, some distance apart.

You have to be careful when introducing a new horse to an established herd. Horses are hierarchical. There is an alpha mare, and a clear understanding among the members of the herd of the status of each horse under her. Sometimes, a lower horse will challenge a more dominant horse, and the balance of power changes. But it can be dicey, and real injury can result. Hooves, shod or not, are hard and sharp, and a horse's jaws are powerful enough to amputate a human limb. So, you have to be careful.

For this operation, the other three mares were contained in the bigger area and everyone was watching us over the fence, curious, but quiet. Chey walked over to a hay feeder and took a bite, then looked up at her new roommates with hay dribbling from her mouth. "I think it'll be all right. I'm going to let the others in," said Louise. She walked down and opened the gate, and the other mares walked up slowly and congregated around the feeder to eat. Chey respectfully moved over a few steps to the other feeder, keeping it between her and the others. Everyone was watching everyone else, and so far, everyone was being polite. There was plenty to eat here, and lots of room, which helped. No competition for food or space.

It was going to be OK. I heaved a big sigh and looked at Celia. She was beaming. "I. Am. So. Proud. Of. You!" she said, as she grabbed me in a big bear hug. I was proud of me, too.

Chapter Two had actually begun.

Chapter Two

After we got Chey to Redmount on a Friday, I went to see her every day, and it appeared to me that it would be getting worse before it got better. Horses are creatures of habit, as are we. Change is always difficult, for any of us. And horses are far more dependent upon their community than most humans are. As prey animals, they evolved to be in a herd that can bond together to fight off predators. Being alone and friendless is more frightening to a horse than it is to us. And horses never know when they step into a horse trailer if they will ever see home and family again. They may not. It happens to almost all of them, at least once in their lives. It was stressful enough for me, and I *knew* what was going on. All Chey knew was every-thing was different, and she wasn't sure where she would be safe.

Her pasture mates were not aggressive, just establishing hier-archy, as one expects in a herd. Chey hadn't lived in a herd for years. She had had her own paddock at Ridgehollow. She had to find her place in the hierarchy of the new herd, and she would be anxious until she did. Little dings and divots began to appear on her honey hide as Jewel and the other mares used their teeth to put her in her place.

She was most tense when I took her out of her paddock. This herd may not have completely accepted her yet, but she was hanging on to it for comfort. I brought her up to the ring to try to do some work with her, but she was so "up," I could barely keep her attention. It would clearly be a while before I'd feel comfortable riding her. But then again, it was eighteen degrees that day, the coldest it'd been in daylight yet that year, and I was sure (I was hoping) that that was contributing to how "up" she was.

So, I decided to take it slow. If the catchphrase for Chapter One had been "taking off the rose-colored glasses," Chapter Two was going to be "do what you can, not what you can't." In other words, don't get hurt.

Meanwhile, back at Ridgehollow, Kay asked if I could help her out and trailer Theo to a veterinarian about forty minutes away in Norwalk. It would save her the cost of the barn call. At this point, I had driven the trailer with a horse in it twice: The first time I ever drove it loaded was to take Debbie's horse to his new home. The second time was to take Chey to hers. "Um . . . sure," I said. I knew Theo, being originally from the track, would load easily, and that is usually the most difficult part. I met her at the farm, she rode, and put Theo in the aisle to untack him and get him ready. I noticed a couple of things. One, Theo was distressed. Horses will poop when they're nervous, and he pooped about six times while he was on the crossties as she unsaddled and unbridled him. Then, I noticed the weather had changed. The sun was gone behind a blanket of clouds, the day had gotten gray, and it had started to drizzle.

"Kay," I said, "maybe this is not a good idea. Maybe we should do this another day." "Naah, it'll be all right, and besides, this vet is a specialist and it's impossible to get an appointment with her." I really did not feel good about this, but I figured, she's had horses for decades, she must know better.

A word about horse trailers. These are essentially big metal boxes used to transport horses. There are lots of styles, but most horse trailers have "butt bars" and "breast bars." The butt bar hangs vertically at the back of the trailer until it is locked into place horizontally after the horse is in, it prevents the horse from backing out, although that's more of suggestion because a really determined horse could probably bust it. The breast bar is a fixed horizontal bar that limits the horse's forward motion in the trailer. There is a space in front of the breast bar to hang hay for the horse to eat in transit, and maybe store a trunk or some tools. Usually, the owner leads the horse in, and a helper stands behind to do up the butt bar. Kay got Theo, whose head was higher that it ought to be, and started walking to the horse trailer. He hesitated a couple of times, but she wrapped the lead line *around her hands* and headed in. She ducked under the breast bar, let go of the lead line to put it *over* the breast bar, and wrapped it around her hands again—both of them. This is not recommended practice. Here's why.

Theo got halfway into the trailer and decided he was not into this. He popped back and hustled out of the trailer. We heard a howl from Kay. She was caught in front of the breast bar. That tug took all the slack out of the lead line, and it seized into a half hitch around her hands. She couldn't let go, and she couldn't move toward the horse to release the pressure, because she was on the other side of the fixed metal bar. And the horse just wanted to get out of the trailer. When he felt resistance, he got scared and pulled harder.

With a force of 1,200 pounds, the nylon lead line cut through flesh like butter. It amputated a finger on her left hand and almost three fingers on her right, which hung by skin alone.

At first, I didn't know what happened and went to catch Theo. Then Kay screamed, "My hands! My hands!" I dropped Theo's lead line and screamed for the barn help to come get him and ran to Kay. Good old Lisa flew out of the barn, got the horse put away, and then, while I took Kay by the shoulders and got her into her car, Lisa found the amputated finger in the wood shavings on the floor of my horse trailer. She put it in a bag of ice, which she draped over Kay's hands, which were now in her lap. She covered it all with the cleanest rag she could find in the tack room, and I drove Kay's car like a demon to Putnam Hospital Center. I waited there until her husband and son showed up.

They were able to re-attach the three fingers on the right hand, but the one that the lead line completely severed could not be re-attached. Kay's husband drove me back to the barn (my truck was there, still attached to the trailer). Lisa had considerately closed it up against the rain, which was now coming down heavily. Everyone gathered to hear the story from me. One of other boarders spit out, "I think your horse trailer is *cursed*!" Which was the last thing I needed to hear just then.

With my heart in my throat, I got into my truck, put it in tow/haul mode, adjusted the brake, and pulled my empty horse trailer back home. I got it halfway up the driveway. I stopped, opened the door, and fell out face-first onto the grass. I had held it together as long as I could. I wasn't going to park it in its space tonight.

Kay's accident was one of those events so significant that it winds up binding a community. The accident . . . the first two or three days when it's all anyone talked about, filling in details, shaking their heads . . . and then, the long tail-off of difficult emotions and bad dreams. My confidence has been improving overall up to then. This was a setback.

It was the first challenge in a succession of them. Scary times with Chey: When I first took her out to work with her in the new ring, I knew I had no control, and I was so scared I let her go. She ran maniacally around the ring, breaking a jump as she soared over it, lead line trailing. Then the first few times I rode her on the trail, she acted up. My anxiety prevented me from dealing with it safely, but Celia was there for me to help me through it. When she came for our first lesson at Redmount, she asked, "Do you want me to lunge her?" "N-n-no," I stuttered. I really did; I was afraid. But I felt this was something I had to work through. She watched me, coached me as I lunged her, turned her, and handled her. I could hand the anxiety over to Celia and focus on the job at hand, and so far, it had worked. I realized how safety depends upon a number of things, but certainly primary among them is, how well you understand what the horse is telling you, and how fast you figure it out. Isn't it funny? That's just what we expect of them. We want them to get good and fast at understanding us. We should take our share in the equation and strive to get better and faster at understanding *them*. For now, I could count on Celia to advise me appropriately. I hoped the day would come when she wouldn't have to.

2012

So the new year came, and with it, winter. Between bronchitis and tension with J, I'd only gotten to the barn every other day, but in this place, that was no neglect of Chey. She was very happy now in her little herd, and with all the hay she could eat, she was passing the time comfortably. I was not sure I liked that she was less dependent upon me. It used to be I felt she looked forward to our time together. Lately, not so much. It was hard to push against the cold, which has become very difficult for me, her reluctance, and J.

And my family. What was left of it.

I mentioned I have a sister, older than me. I remember, as a child, tagging along on dates and visiting her at college in DC, and in her first NYC apartment, being appropriately impressed at her grown-up-ness. Then, she got a master's degree in social work, and everybody was impressed. But things changed.

Beginning in 1978, about the time I was leaving the arts and heading toward night school, she slipped down some stairs entering a town house. That event marked the beginning of an almost unbroken succession of injuries, illnesses, syndromes, symptoms, and conditions. Mom never left her side as the complaints accelerated, going with her to innumerable doctor visits and accompanying her to uncounted treatment venues. They were never able to present a diagnosis—I remember that early on, MS was suggested as an explanation for the symptoms, but when a test for MS was developed, it proved not to be the case. After a few years of this, the family began to raise their eyebrows, but Mom stood by her, defended her, and supported her all the way. I had begun my Wall Street whirlaway by then, and the hours I worked excused me in Mom's mind from participating much in this.

My sister once worked for the New York City Department of Finance, but that trickled down as the incapacities increased. The city offered her a buyout at some point, when she wasn't showing up for work regularly (she was a civil servant at a high enough level, she couldn't be fired). She took it.

As I mentioned, living with Mom's version of love was not easy. My sister came in for it, too, although she says I got the worst of it. My sister had conflicted feelings about being virtually dependent upon Mom.

I had reconciled with Mom and had a pretty good relationship with her toward the end. Not so, my sister. Even when our mom was in her eighties, she was still going to my sister's apartment to help out with the laundry, cooking, and shopping. On those occasions when I was there, my sister could hardly wait until Mom was out of the room before she started venting to me about her. I felt this was terribly unjust to Mom, who, while difficult, never failed her: so, while as a child I had the typical adoring view of my older sister, after the fall, we didn't have a rewarding relationship.

I always figured my sister'd come around at the end. It didn't happen. I was the one with Mom when she went into the coma. The next day, my sister and I were heading out to the hospital together. We hired a car, since she doesn't take subways or trains (traveling on a train would develop a "plaque on the brain," she explained). It was her first time seeing Mom after the stroke. En route, my sister felt it necessary to stop at Mom's house to get the good jewelry. I was stunned. "For safekeeping," she said. The car waited while we went inside.

The stroke happened the day before and this was the first time either of us was in the house since. It was as if Mom knew her time had come, because when we got in, we saw that the house she loved was meticulous, bed made, dishes washed and put away, even the garbage pails were empty. As if above all else, Mom wanted to be remembered as a good housekeeper, a pursuit in which she took tremendous pride. My sister charged into Mom's bedroom and tugged the drawers out of her dresser, dumping the contents on the bed and floor, grabbing fistfuls of necklaces and rings and shoving them into her purse. "What are you doing?" I cried. "It doesn't matter now, does it?" she replied.

Mom's death hit me hard. My sister appeared less stricken and she took care of all the funeral arrangements with efficiency. After shiva, I was so distressed, I felt I needed to be near horses. "Go, go!" she said. "It'll be good for you!" I spent three days in California with a horse friend, who took wonderful care of me. When I returned, my sister had all but emptied the house, discarding furniture, linens, china, kitchenware, mementos. She had neither asked nor told me her intentions. Perhaps she thought it is what I assumed she would do. She seemed proud of herself for getting so much done in my absence. I was bereft. It may not have been a totally happy childhood, but I would have liked the chance to say good-bye to it; and, with the house upstate, I would have liked to have some of the stuff, just as mementos. "Well, if you wanted anything, you should have told me," she said. To be fair, she shared the jewels and any money from the sale of the furniture with me.

She made an effort to keep in touch, as did I.

But, bottom line: although we shared many of the same experiences, we were not close, and she was not in a position to help me through my emotional problems, which were, as I have mentioned, enormous. There were aunts and uncles and cousins who were well-meaning and kind, but they were growing their own families. They commended my mother and me on my return to school and my progress up the corporate ladder, were happy to see us at the bar mitzvahs and later on, the weddings; but they had their own families to focus on, and my needs were bottomless. While remaining friendly, we grew more distant over the years, as children and grandchildren happily filled out their lives.

After a Hannukah visit to the city, and a little time off for Cheyenne, I rode her the next day, and the next. I was amazed. It was as if she had been thinking about all the stuff we do for the little hiatus she got when we changed barns. She was so good and calm, it was a pleasure, and reminded me, after this challenging few weeks, what is so wonderful about having a good relationship with a horse. When I was with her, I often thought of the song, "You raise me up so I can stand on mountains . . ." She really did. It was a pleasure to ride her, be with her. It gave me a lift that lasted all day, and made me feel like keeping on doing something physical and outdoorsy. It was just me and Chey, in a pre-digital time, in world of scents and vision and mind and muscle, it is an animal thing between us, not a human one, and I really loved it. It appeared to be good for me.

Winters had become more challenging for me; perhaps it was just that for my whole life until then I spent most of them indoors. I got sick, dependably, almost all winter. If I waited to feel better to ride, I wouldn't, so I pushed myself, trusting that even at half-mast, Chey wouldn't hurt me. I had become sensitive to the feel, in a deeper way that could only come as my increasing trust in this horse. And she was a willing partner in that. What could be better? I realized that my horsemanship and my overall emotional health were completely dependent upon each other. The way I used to cope with anxiety, stress, depression, was to smoke, eat, and drink. The more time I spent with horses, the better I felt about myself. The better I felt about myself, the more I enjoyed my life and its opportunities, and the better I was about making healthier choices for myself. Things were not perfect, but they were getting better. If I wanted to ride the next day, I couldn't drink too much. If I wanted to be strong enough to go to Chey, I needed to continue to eat thoughtfully. If I wanted to have energy for Chey, I needed to keep up with the gym. Feeling good about myself was still so new. I wished I could feel that way all the time.

The relationship with J was not good. Had been house hunting. Hadn't seen anything as nice as the house he and I shared. After a hiatus, I began lessons again. Celia had been banging on Chey terribly, telling me she was a lousy horse, not athletic, not well trained, not good-natured. She kept telling me, "You gotta get rid of her and get a good horse. You'll never be any better until you do." She really leaned into me, and I left the lesson feeling crushed and downhearted and miserable and the feeling stuck around all week. Then I called a cousin, with whom I thought I had a good relationship (she always used my apartment when she

159

came to the city) to talk about buying J out of his share of the property. But she had no patience: She had heard it all before. I wouldn't want to own the property because it would be such a tremendous financial strain and such a tremendous amount of work . . . Then, to change the subject and in search of something positive, I told her proudly that after thirty years and four or five tries, I had finally succeeded and quit smoking. "It's about time!" she said. Sigh.

It turned February, and my fifty-ninth birthday arrived. I had occasion to reflect at how well pleased I was with most aspects of my life. What a pleasant state to be in. My sister called to wish me well, and ask how I felt about almost being sixty. "It's wonderful," I said. "This life is not always easy, but I am doing what I love, and am excited about the choices I have." "Well," she said. "And what about all the choices you no longer have?"

That statement made me stop in my tracks. It was so typical of the way I used to think about things, how I would only see the "can't," see where I failed, missed, lost, erred, and/or disappointed. And in a flash, I saw how far I'd come from the negative, self-defeating ways of thinking that had plagued me for most of my life. Something you have a choice about is whether you hold on to ways of thinking that don't serve you, events in the past that damaged you, rose-colored glasses that mislead you. But all I said was, "No. I don't spend any time thinking about that. Why would I?"

After a day off, Chey usually greets me with interest. As in, willing to give me her attention, despite the presence of her field-mates and the hay. She greeted me so today, as if she was pleased to see me. She was unusually calm on the crossties.

When she was like this, she was a lovely horse to be around, and it was especially pleasant to be taking care of her. She was like this more and more these days. I loved her so much.

Next day, it was very cold. I was wearing my chinks and my cowboy hat. Chey had her thick winter coat on, and whereas she looks like burnished bronze in the summer, she looked like a woolly mammoth now. She and I were in the sunshine. Chey had been watching me since she first saw me, and I was really pleased that she continued to pay attention to me, like I was something important. I didn't ask for anything until I was closer, but then stopped, picked my eyes up, and looked at her and put

Winter Wooley

Me and my girl

the thought in my mind, *Come here*. It took a moment or two. Then she turned away from the hay and her friends and took a step or two toward me. I rewarded her immediately with big happiness body, and she leaned toward me as I went to reach her and hug her face.

I put on her halter and we stood there for a while, me caressing her face, she enjoying it, moving with it. Louise was there with a camera and she said, "Oh, you two look so great, and with your chinks and cowboy hat, can I take pictures?" And I said of course, of course. I wonder if those pictures caught anything of what that moment was like, because it was just wonderful.

Then we worked the ring and then went on a walk with one of the other boarders. That day was a good day.

I was telling everyone that I was beginning the last year of middle age. I enjoyed that. Because, you know what came after the Middle Ages, right? The Renaissance. The *Enlightenment*.

Reflections in the
Present Tense I

I find something that works well is focusing on the here and now, and not letting monkey mind take over when I am home alone in the early evenings at the house—my danger time.

One Sunday, an article in the *New York Times Magazine* caught my interest. It talked about habit, about the unconscious choices you make because the pattern of behavior they represent has become so ingrained, that the mind stops participating. Like, when you enter a room that smells like garlic, you smell it, but if you have been cooking in that room, you no longer smell the garlic because your mind has tuned it out. Marketers can exploit that, by recognizing or creating patterns that become self-perpetuating. But people can exploit that, too, to their benefit, by recognizing the machinery of a habit they may want to break; by analyzing the components of the behavior, one can test outcomes one by one, and thereby come at the source event or feeling that makes that habit so hard to break. I no longer smoke, and my drinking is extremely rare. These were among the worst of the habits I brought with me from my prior life, and I am, at the moment, coping fairly well. There's one more I'd really like to break . . .

164

Bodywork

It was an odd day in late February 2012, after an odd winter. We had two feet of snow at the end of October and nothing since until that day. Temperatures dipped to the teens but seemed to hover around forty; and for the second year in a row, I heard thunder at the wrong time of year; last year in January, this year in February. Days that February climbed to near sixty. But finally, there was snow, and as J and I walked our Nuclear Lake loop, a squall kicked up. It wasn't snow and it wasn't hail, but something in between; little points of noncrystalline snow, about the size of the little cotton balls the dentist grasps in his or her instrument.

And I came to explore two things with my mind.

First was collection and extension. J, my human friend, is fully a foot taller than me. Toward the end of the walk, he asked if we could pick up the pace so I tried extending my stride. I paid attention, so I could better understand extension in my horse. I realized that it takes a lot of energy to extend and a lot of freedom of movement. So I'm thinking that I can help Chey better by giving her more energy and thinking about freeing up my own body as well. I began to focus more about how my body could help hers do what I wanted—not just by applying the aids, but by being *myself* what I wanted her to be. Extension requires a different sort of balance than collection, too; it is a faster flow through time, and where there is more energy, you have to be more relaxed to let it flow, or else it will take you with it.

Then, I had some thoughts about J. Our relationship. We had been "together" nineteen years to date because there are important things we like together, like the hiking that has gotten increasingly more modest in exertion over the years. I think that, just like I had certain expectations of him based on where it appeared we were going, I think he had certain expectations of me based on where we'd been. He never expected me to change, but I did as I got healthier, as my self-esteem improved, and as I came to my life with horses. And we were unexpectedly thrust into living together, which was never where we should have gone. We were just hiking, skiing, and occasional event people. We were not meant to live together. Our ideas about the level of chaos and order we need in our lives are radically different. I cannot concentrate if my bed is unmade, or there are dishes in the sink. He can live that way, and therein lies the conflict.

A Setback

One day in March, I went to get Chey and she had a swelling the size of a baseball on her right front leg. I called the vet. He inspected her, palpated her, ultrasounded her. Chey had torn the deep digital flexor tendon in her right front leg, almost all the way through. Given the careful way I ride her, he thought it most probable that she did it to herself, running around the paddock with the other mares. It was a serious tear—and he could not at this point say how she would come out of it. She would be on R & R for a minimum of three months. During the first month, I would have to come morning and evening to ice the leg for twenty minutes, apply a topical anti-inflammatory and standing wraps. Then she needed at least two more months off. After that, the vet would check her again. If she was OK, we could begin rehab. The general rule for rehabilitation is: It takes as long to come back as the period in which the horse was convalescing. If she comes back.

It happens.

Chey was injured. She was my whole life now. I'd given up my job, my paycheck, my health care, my relationship was failing, and now Chey was hurt. This is just the kind of stress that would ordinarily send me into a binge. Food, drink, television. I was in danger.

But then I remembered the *New York Times* article about forming habits and breaking them. It is all related to behavior that has become unconscious or subconscious. Become conscious of it. Break the behavior down step by step. When do you do it? What do you usually do just before? Just before that? I think that if you become aware of the catalyst, or rather catalysts, for the bad behavior, you can make a choice about whether to slide along, or interrupt the chain. So I formed a plan on how to break the pattern:

Don't leave home hungry. Make a point of having lunch, an official lunch. You are allowed to eat.

Drink as much water as you can. If you can't . . .

Drink two or three big glassfuls as soon as you can after getting home, while feeding Odin or starting a fire.

Try to take the course that takes you closer to engagement with your life, and not the one that will result in the opposite.

And this time . . . it worked.

Riding Other Horses

Since I couldn't ride Chey, Celia found another horse she thought it would be good for me to learn on, and I was looking forward to starting lessons again, because I wanted so much to progress in my horsemanship. The horse was Southern Comfort, a sweet quarter horse mare, only five years old. She was barely broke, and very fast, but she had a sweet disposition and I knew Celia wouldn't let me get hurt. So, last week, we gave it a try.

Oh my goodness. Southern Comfort was a crotch rocket! In fact, her barn name was "Rocket." Part of it was her nature, part of it her limited training. I was very anxious on her back, she read it, fed off it, and it was not at all pleasant, flying around, hauling on the reins without gaining any control. "Relax," Celia would say. Easy for you to say! But I knew she was right. My tension was inhibiting my feel and cueing Southern Comfort to go, my hands were braced and pulling against a horse who was bracing back, my back was stiff, my shoulders ached from pulling the reins, and this just wasn't working. "Relax," Celia said.

"You're not coming off. You know how to ride a horse." Yeah, but I also got bucked off my first horse every time I got him, from the day I brought him home. I got slammed off Nifty and added a concussion and a contusion to my trophies. I'm afraid of falling off again. She'd bolt. I'd rise up in my stirrups. "Stay in the saddle," Celia called. "Remember, that's the whole idea! Stay in the saddle. Stay with the horse." John Lyons says, "Remember, you can ride as fast as they can run." But it's hard to relax when you feel you're on the verge of getting launched. However, that is exactly what you have to do. On and on we went, not stopping, I could hardly catch my breath. Celia said, "You know why I don't let you quit, right?" Right. You have to learn to feel the motion, and the only way to do that, is to do that.

We didn't make a lot of progress that day, but progress takes time. Feel takes time. Even if you have to feel what's wrong, that's still progress. Celia seems to have faith that we will get there. It was just that, going fast with this horse was so much faster than I ever went with Chey. It was not comfortable. But Celia gave me a strategy. "When Chey is ready, I want you to lope a lot." That was like being told to spend a day in a candy store. Sure, I love loping. But then I realized what she was getting at. Riding Chey fast: There's a point to it besides being fun. It's not fun riding Southern Comfort because I'm not used to going that fast. How does one get used to it? By doing it!

I had also been riding Mikky. Mikky is a beautiful big dappled gray, and I forget his precise genealogy, but there was Arabian and warmblood in some combination, which made him really handsome. But he had some issues. He scared me. When Celia would get on him, she instantly put him into the bridle and he cantered along, beautifully rounded. Then I'd get on, and he was a different horse. I got used to loping along, relaxing into his stride, got the feel for him. Once he was loosened up, he was wonderful. I rode him for several lessons. My heels eased down; my hands got lower. I was able to sit on him. I even took him over a cavaletti or two. And he was such a beautiful horse. You can tell, even while on board. There is something extra nice about riding a beautiful horse.

Another Setback

Chey was off the twice-a-day therapy, I was back to going to the barn once a day to feed her and groom her, although we were not riding yet. Then, my back went out, as it does periodically. I had had some impressive accidents during my summers in Wyoming that resulted in visits to the Washakie Medical Center. Then, that year with Shammes, when my fifty-four-year-old body hit the dirt with daily regularity, had taken its toll. When my back goes, it goes. I had to remain largely motionless with ice then heat on and off my back. This happens frequently, and I have neat little cold packs in stockings, so I can tie them on and move a little while keeping the cold on. J's been pretty good and even driven me once to the barn to feed Chey *without* a bribe. Even carried a couple of things for me.

A few days later, it was so bad I asked J to take me to the emergency room, and after wrangling about taking my vehicle or his, we took his car. A steroid shot and some Vicodin, added to the two massages I'd had, plus the heat and cold, seems to have bro-

172

ken through to someplace meaningful in my back. My mood was measurably brighter. I told him, "I know we don't always get along, but when I have an emergency, you have been there to help me. I'll try to remember that more." He said, "Well, I could see you needed help . . ."

The first day of spring arrived, and daffodils were up all over. I wondered how many of ours (I mean, I guess I should say "mine") would come up that year. I would like to plant some more daffodils.

Riding for the Brand

At about that time, I began riding for Celia. I'm her turn-back guy, and general ranch hand. I show up at her place between 7:30 and 8:00 a.m., and by now, we had a routine: Take out the three cutting horses and the old usin' horse,[4] which I would ride, to move cattle and turn back. The usin' horse, Zip, was a semi-retired pro, solid as the rock of Gibraltar. He looked like the strongest cow horse you've ever seen. In fact, he might be. He knew his job (in fact, he was teaching *me* the job) and he never took a wrong step, or spooked or bucked since I had known him. They gave him to me, because they didn't want me to get hurt, and they knew this good horse would take care of me, unless I did something stupid, and maybe even then.

4. "Usin' horse" is a cowboy term for a good solid horse you "use" for the general chores. For example, you wouldn't use a cutting horse to round up the cattle, you would just use him for cutting. The "usin' horse" is the one who gets the cows and keeps them in line so the cutting horse can do his thing.

174

Back to our routine: I groom; Celia mucks stalls. Her horses spend most of the day in their stalls, and the muck buckets can weigh more than sixty pounds, which proved to be too much for me to repeatedly lift over my head to empty into the Dumpster they keep for the purpose. Celia, as I mentioned, is quite a big woman, and younger than me, and can manage it a little more easily. At that point, I knew which horse got which saddle and which pad. She would use her saddle on two of the cutting horses, so I would make sure it was adjusted correctly for the one she would start with. We used to use the "usin'" saddle on the horse I'd ride, but those stirrups didn't go short enough for me, so I would just bring my saddle and use that. Celia and Kyle had about forty bridles with different bits; different bits have different effects, and different horses have different preferences, so the selection of that day's bridle was not random. I knew which bridle went with "my" horse, and Celia would tell me what to get for the others. I knew their names: the correctional, the grazer, the double-hinged port.

She would take a couple of horses and the bucket with the boots that protect the horse's lower legs and bottles of water up to the ring, I would bring a couple of horses, and her husband would follow riding the other usin' horse. We would leave the prep area (where we groom, tack up, and hose off the horses afterward) and go through a gate into the holding field. Then there's the arena in which she would cut. Then, the field holding the cows. He and I would chip off five cows from the herd and move them through a gate into the arena. Then we would put them into position in the arena. Celia would work three cows, as one would in a show. After each group, when she was done, we would open the gate to the holding field and move the cows into it. She would take the boots off the cutting horse and give him to me, and I would walk him out, leading him while

175

riding Zip (this is called ponying) until he quit blowing. Then, I would take them down, through the holding field, through a gate, to the showers.

I had gotten to where I pony the horses not only in the ring but, very carefully, back down through the holding field containing loose cows. These calves were fresh, meaning they hadn't had a lot of contact with horses or humans, and they were very jumpy, so you would need to be very quiet and slow when you moved two cow horses, whose job was to chase them, through them. It would be several hours of physically demanding work, and I had never been happier.

Thanks to Zip, I came to understand something about horses versus pets. That big strong animal lent me his strength and speed, but it was only a loan. He was not a pet. He was a working animal, a partner. To think of them as pets did not put you in a place of proper respect. And you always needed to respect your horse. Pets live in our homes, sleep in our beds. They live in our world. Horses do not. When we engage with horses, it has to be on their terms. Celia said it often, "They are not pets. They are horses." I thought I finally understood what she meant. It doesn't mean you can't love them, but the relationship needs to be appropriate.

The relationship needs to be appropriate. How much of my life has been unsatisfying or downright disappointing because I did not have the right relationship with people, meaning, the right expectations of what I should offer and what I could expect? How could I? I was seeing what I hoped was there and not what was there.

After we rode at Celia's house, we would go to Connecticut where she "tunes" a couple of horses for clients. The client, Jason, who owned the place was a big name in cutting, on the board of the National Cutting Horse Association (NCHA), and had a cutting horse and a usin' horse on the property. I had been riding the usin' horse, Cloudy. He was a cute little five-year-old, ranch-bred and broke quarter horse purchased out West. Dappled gray, hence, the name. He, unlike Chey, was *not* the kind of horse you could just get on and ride, unless you spent your spare time riding saddle broncs, but after some lunging and work, he was OK.

I just loved it. I worked four to six hours a day for her, for free, for the chance to ride these horses and work cattle on them. Celia pounded on me every minute she wasn't actually cutting, and I got open sores on my sit bones that I daily tried to salve and bandage, but I always showed up and I always rode, leaving blood on the saddle from time to time. It was incredibly painful, but Celia just kept pounding and I just kept riding. I wasn't going to miss an opportunity. Cowboy up.

Reflections in the
Present Tense II

Along the lines of breaking habits: Some habits are not bad. Lighting candles to me just makes for such a warm and welcoming environment that I always want to do it. Trying to get into the habit of washing my hands at some point shortly after I get home from the barn. Before I feed Odin, preferably. Deciding to encourage writing instead of overindulging on some available substance. I am trying to replace the reflexive behavior with conscious behavior. I know this is a good thing.

I feel sometimes I am getting lazy, that I could be doing so much more with Chey. But I also found that when the fun goes out of it, it stops being productive. Or even pleasant. And I understand more and more about myself through my relationship with that horse. One of my greatest needs is for the ability to tell when enough is enough when it comes to pushing myself. It took tenacious push to get me where I am today—to this absolute Candy Land of horses. I never would have believed it, back then. Never. I wanted to die so many times.

Perhaps it is actually better if I stop pushing now. My life is different now. I have a relationship with this lovely mare. She recognizes me and follows me. I've never had that before. I've had so few fully trusting relationships in my life, human or otherwise. This feeling of *I am with you*. I feel as though this kind mare is helping me to gently learn how to be a better human.

Better Habits

I decided to go to the Authors' Night at the library. I believed widening my circle would be a good move in connection with feeling lonely, so I took the opportunity.

I was really tired after the gym, episodes of *Law and Order* were end-to-end on cable, and Odin was lying on me. And . . . I had done some planting when I got home. It was so comfortable on the couch with Odin. But I got up, put on some makeup, and dressed nicely in a rose-colored long sleeve crew and the carpenter's jeans that hang low. And a new haircut, and the makeup and all . . . I was prepared to sit out a lot of this meeting, not talk, just listen. They did offer the opportunity to ask questions, though, and I took it.

And . . . I was coming to a new position on horses, too. I was growing to where I could see that Chey's discomfort in some situations was not typical of all horses, and that it was possible to have a horse who was already good at whatever it was. Not every horse can do every thing. It didn't diminish Chey. There were just some things that she wasn't good at, through no fault of her own. It was all right. It occurred to me that the same thing applied for me, too. There were some things I was not good at. I was not a bad person because of it. There is no moral value to your talents or lack of them.

I was beginning to think there might be a "next" horse. A horse who could take me further. If I was thinking like that, I realized, I needed to decide where I wanted to go.

Reflections in the
Present Tense III

I am watching Dr. Wayne Dyer, and he has said some things I
want to remember: How would it feel if you had those things
or were those things that you want to be? Loved, accomplished,
admired? Imagine how that would feel, and *feel it right now.*
Give those feelings your subjective attention: Don't let what
anyone else says or thinks interfere with those feelings.

Then he just spontaneously repeated a stream of dahs and dits
representing the verbal presentation of Morse code, A to Z. He
said, he learned that fifty-three years ago, and here it was. Lesson: Some of the stuff you have carried with you is harmless,
like knowing Morse code, but some of it is much more damag-
ing, like Mom's disapproval. You can let it go.

Let It Go

I had to say good-bye to Odin on April 14, 2012. I knew it wouldn't be long when I got him: He was old and he was FIV positive. I took him because I knew no one would want this aging cat, and no one *could* take him who had other cats. It was time, but it's always hard. It was so short, just a year and change. Seemed like much longer. He was such a nice creature to be around. Been there, done that, but still kind to humans. I really liked him, he had such personality, and I came to care for him even though he was polite but reserved with me. Toward the end, he got a little cozier; sleeping on me if I was lying on the couch, sitting on the blanket on my lap when I had morning coffee. He was a good cat for dozing with, but then again, isn't any cat?

I realize the house seems lonely without a cat.

My mouth still hurts from that hammering root canal last Monday and between the swelling on my right side, and the hole in my left side from the tooth that was extracted in January, it's hard to chew and my diet has gone to pot. I'm eating what I can, not what I should, and that has been ice cream, sour cream, yogurt, and pasta. Not feeling strong.

I also missed mornings and evenings with Chey. It was awfully nice to see her twice a day even though the reason was her torn tendon was in the acute phase and I was treating it. What a lovely horse. I miss spending more time with her. What can I do with her that does not involve much locomotion? That was the challenge.

In the meantime, I went to Putnam Humane, and adopted another pair of older cats. Pippie and Twinkie. Welcome home.

Something good was happening between me and J.

One weekend, I had told him that I wanted to go to an NCHA event in Pennsylvania, in which Celia was a participant, and I might stay over. I wasn't sure what I'd do and didn't feel like planning anything, because it was hard losing Odin. He, out of the blue, suggested he would come with me. "But you'll be bored out of your skull!" I said. He said no; he'd bring a book and take a walk. He was good to his word. We didn't leave quite as early as I'd hoped, but I didn't miss anything, and he didn't complain, and he even brought one of his little radios so he didn't burn out my truck battery listening to the radio for six hours. He stopped by the ring briefly, made an appearance, and then, a little earlier than I'd planned, we headed home but again, I didn't miss anything. He wanted to stop at Long John Silver's (funny, the buyout of Long John Silvers in the 1980s was a deal I was involved in) to pick up dinner, and I was elated from the experience of the horse show, and since he had been so good, I didn't mind. I drove the four-hundred-mile round-trip all by myself.

I was glad to have him along.

Milestones

I didn't really want to ride Rocket ever again. What happened?

One thing, my gym routine and diet had really slacked off. The month I had to go to Chey morning and afternoon for her wraps interfered with my Monday-Wednesday-Friday gym schedule. Then, the dental work interfered with my diet. I guessed it was not unreasonable, that you wouldn't want to ride if you were not feeling well or strong. So I figured, the more I could get to the gym, the better I would eat and sleep, the more ready I would be to ride.

Another major milestone. I decided to give up the apartment in the city. I had held on to it all this time, because it sounded so cool to say "and I have an apartment in the city." But I wasn't using it, the trip down to pay the rent took a day away from riding, and I was pretty certain that I wasn't going back. I thought about it awhile. I knew that if I gave up that rent-stabilized, four hundred square feet on Carmine Street, I would never be able to afford to live in the city again. Was I ready? Really, really ready?

I wasn't sure, but I decided it was time, whether or not I was ready. In May 2012, I took the last trip down with the truck. J came along. Piled in the last of the stuff I am taking. All that was left was to turn in the keys.

I felt a strange mix of emotions. Sure, it was time, and I had a much better life now, but it was also a true commitment to my new life. It is a country life, and I realized that there were things about city life that, to be honest, I liked. I'd loved acting, dancing, singing, and being around that milieu. There is a subtext of speech and body language that is different in the city from the country. That knowledge was bothering me, and I realized why. It was trying to make me anxious about this next big change, because that was my old default position trying to ascend. But really, I wasn't losing anything. I still had my life of almost sixty years there. Yeah, baby, I was cool, and opting for a very different kind of life now took nothing from that, and if anything, made me even more cool. I was even beginning to feel that way about me, myself. Yeah. I was pretty cool.

So now, it was another beginning. Who would I be now and for the rest of my life? I was finding out things about myself. Good things. Maybe it was the horses helping me to see in ways I never could before. Could I be the person I'd had glimpses of in this, my new life?

Depression is like a dictator, whose only interest is in self-perpetuation. You retreat deeply into yourself, tightly holding your defenses. Everything is a threat, and you have nothing with which to defend yourself. Now, I am finding out . . .

That I am genuinely engaged in trying to do healthy things regarding tobacco, alcohol, food, and exercise, to the degree I can . . .

That I can look for a connection with another living thing, and if I am attentive, I can see how to achieve it . . .

That my days now seem to be a lot about taking care of things, plants, and animals.

It appeared in this odd way, I had chosen a kind of motherhood, a term I despised for so long because to me it represented unending self-denial in the service of unappreciative offspring. But I realized then, as I was working in the gardens and selecting a rosebud to bring in to the house, that when you care about something or someone, it can be a pleasure to take care of it. I enjoyed taking care these things I loved. My horse, my cats, and now . . . what would be my house. Perhaps next, I would look forward to taking care of me.

Two Steps Forward . . .
Back One

I had a horrible dream. I was on a bike ride with J; he was on a motorcycle. He pulled ahead and I lost him. I got frantic, trying to figure out where I was. I had the two cats with me on my bike, and, for some reason, my saddle. I was getting more and more frantic. Finally, I tried to call home to leave a message, but my phone was different. I couldn't figure out how to use it, and every time I pressed a key, the wrong thing came up on the screen. My shoes wouldn't tie; my saddle, my cats, my bike, and my clothes were all stolen. I finally rushed into a store yelling for help, and they were just casual about it. . . . . What a horrible anxiety dream! Who is it in my head who hates me that much?

I had been very irritated with J, his lack of forethought, his carelessness. How many times does he have to be told not to put wet cups or glasses on the wooden shelf over the sink? He'd ruined at least two wood surfaces so far.

I was anticipating a real argument about the weed whacker. I used it to keep some of the more difficult areas of the property under control, and finally, it gave out. It spun, but not fast enough or strong enough to cut anything. I expected him to go the same way he has with the tractor or the lawn mowers. "Oh, they have to 'rest.' You can't use them steadily." I was prepared to tell him, I cannot take care of this property with tools that can't be used to do the job they're meant for. I was prepared to tell him to buy me out, because under his philosophy, the value of the property will do nothing but decline.

I stopped short of having an argument I knew would be unproductive. I happened to notice it was the seventh anniversary of My New Life, August 28, 2013. My last day as a banker had been back in 2006.

I had been feeling very vague for a few days. Not really tuned in, floaty, couldn't make up my mind about what to do. I realized that I had also been off caffeine for the last few days. I shut it off, because I was no longer sleeping. I was sleeping better, but I really did not like the state of semi-awareness. I had added back one scoop of caff, mixed in with three scoops of decaf, and felt so much better . . . But a few days later, I had a very bad time of it. Nightmares.

Chapter Three

Things are going great with Celia and Rocket. I was quite frightened of this horse; she was faster than an Irish clog dancer. For a long time, I was seriously hindered by fear, but now, I was really beginning to feel things, like her hind legs, and when she was inverting. She was a *very* challenging horse, but I thought when I could ride her, it would be a significant step in the right direction. I drove to Flemington, New Jersey, by myself to watch Celia's show (she did great, placed in one event I was there for). Monday, Ellen and I planned to trailer the horses to Red Wing, about three miles away, for a trail ride. And it was a wonderful experience for me and Chey. Pete, Ellen's unflappable gelding, got in the trailer first, and Chey clearly was alarmed at the prospect of joining him, but I had learned so much from her: It *has* to be the horse's decision, and you have to give the horse the time she needs to make that decision. Ellen was great. She just stood by, didn't speak, didn't suggest using food, didn't want to get a whip or a rope, and after just a few minutes, Chey tucked in her tuppenny and walked in. She was calm in the trailer, got out, ground-tied while I saddled her up, and we had a great ride. The wooden bridge was no problem at all. Going back, it took about half as long for her to decide to get in. "Chapter Three has begun!" I chimed, triumphantly, to Ellen. I was so proud of my wonderful horse.

So why did I have that terrible nightmare that night about getting carjacked at knifepoint, so real I could feel the knife against my throat. And when I escaped and got back to the car to try to get away, the steering wheel had been removed. It shook the hell out of me, and I woke up in a terror. I binged bad that day and the next.

Celia steadied me. I had my lesson on Rocket the next day, and I told Celia what was going on in my head, and she knew just how to push me. Not speed, but refinement, working on getting Rocket into the bridle. I could feel it happening, and it was wonderful. I couldn't *make* it happen, but I could *let* it happen. What an incredible understanding about horsemanship! A little this, a little that, it was never just one thing, but what seemed to matter most was your mind. My mind was making it happen with Rocket. What an amazing thing.

It was September 11, 2012. Perhaps the great significance of this day had reached its climax on the ten-year anniversary in 2011. And while we continued to remember, and respect, and grieve, the wound was healing and we were moving on. There's a lot to be said for moving on. . . .

During the lesson with Celia, she asked me to lope Rocket and I said, "No, please no!" I was so scared. So we talked about it, and I loped a few strides and then said, "Hey! That wasn't so bad."

I noticed something: It was the first time in my life where what was on my mind and what I wanted to do had a greater draw than what was on television. Television used to be the absolute nucleus, the guilty pleasure I was addicted to, the safe retreat from my unpleasant life, a chance to escape. Now, I had a life with horses, and for the first time, I didn't want to escape. I wanted to be here.

Maybe that was part of the Thing. When I didn't need to escape, I wouldn't need the Thing.The bingeing. *Hmmm.*

Anyway, I'd spent three hours working on my horse trailer, cleaning it, sweeping it, pulling up the mats, washing the windows. The next day, I planned to take Ellen and Pete and Chey and me on a trail ride to someplace new—Freedom Park—and *I* would be trailering us in *my* horse trailer. Chapter Three.

I had once said to Celia that I realized it would take a lot of work to get Chey comfortable with the horse trailer. Celia said it wouldn't take that much work. She was right. It didn't take nearly as much work as I thought it would. It would be the third time she has been in a horse trailer since I've owned her, the second time she would enter it for a lark and not a permanent change of address. She was being just wonderful, still timid but trusting enough to finally get on. I had come to love this horse even more after riding Rocket. I had come back to Chey with the understanding that I was not going to fall off. Rocket was making me so much braver, and I saw that while Chey may not been a barrel horse or a cutting horse, she was a wonderful trail horse. There you go. Bob's your uncle.

And I really had a horse and I really had a truck and a horse trailer and this was really happening.

Buck

I had the opportunity to attend a Buck Brannaman clinic with a friend from the barn who was taking her horse. You may have heard of Buck: He was one of the inspirations for the character of Tom Booker in *The Horse Whisperer,* and in fact, Buck did all the actual round pen work in that film. Cindy Meehl's documentary about his life, *Buck*, has become very popular. In a nutshell, he is a man who survived an incredibly brutal childhood. He knows what it feels like, to have to perform under threat of pain if you fail. Rather than perpetuate that on the horses he works with, he has taken a very different course. "Let the horse not be troubled," he says. It is good advice for anyone, of any species.

I got back from the clinic with lots to think about. Brannaman is very charismatic. Very tall, six foot four maybe, kind. When he talks with you, it's like standing in the sun. He gives you his entire attention. He is all about softness and quality. If it isn't good, don't worry about the next thing, just stay there and get it good. Because if it's bad, good can't come from bad. So . . . get it good.

Something happened that I never would have thought possible. When I came back from the clinic, I went to get Chey to practice some of the stuff I learned. I could tell, I was not all there, and she was displeased with what I was asking. Perhaps waking her up from a five-day nap and asking some of this of her was not really fair. I got on her, and to my amazement, I was disappointed.

I immediately chastised myself. I had no cause to be disappointed with this horse. Chey has always given me the best she could. I tried to be more respectful, and she responded. I believed I was forgiven. However, it told me I was really progressing and was recognizing her more for what she is. It didn't mean I loved her any the less, but it did mean I was moving ahead. I was seeing what was, not what I wanted to see. I was OK with this. She had done so much for me; everyone who knows me could see that. However, I see I have grown in horsemanship. It is permitted to recognize that there is more. Wanting to go further doesn't negate any of it. And it may be I've reached the same place with J. I could recognize it better, because of Chey. Recognize what you have. Appreciate it. It is permitted to want more.

It was November 2012. The Year of the Perfect Storm. Hurricane Sandy collided with a winter storm coming in from the West, intersecting an arctic air mass descending from the north, on a full moon. The hurricane made landfall in New Jersey and sent a fourteen-foot wall of water up New York Harbor. The subways were indeed submarine, as were the tunnels into Manhattan. I had spent most of my life traveling those subway lines downtown, and I was shocked at the pictures. Had I been in them that day, the water would have been over my head. This was the biggest storm to hit since ever.

Upstate, there were twenty-four horses at the farm, and Louise wanted to get them out of the weather. Horses like these, who have been living outdoors, have sturdy shelter and all the hay they want to eat, are pretty durable. But with hurricane force winds, anything can happen, and she was taking no chances. She set up panels in the big box stalls, making two straight stalls out of each, and we got all the horses into the barn. Chey, as far as I know, had never lived in a stall but always lived outdoors where she could roam freely. I didn't know how she'd handle this. It helped that all her friends were coming in, too. As the winds roared and the rain pelted, they stood there in their straight stalls for two days, good as gold. A number of us showed up that second day to take everyone out, clean the stalls, re-bed them, change the waters, and put the horses back in. They had plenty to eat and buckets of water, and their friends, and it worked out just fine. The next day, Chey was a little stocked up, but as soon as she got back outside and could move around, her fetlocks tightened up.

It was quite a storm. I lost power at the house. I was not uncomfortable: Candlelight and silence suit me. After a few days, I started running short of water, but I had plenty of heat from the wood stove and lots of food. Gasoline deliveries were delayed, and I thought of all the places in the world where gas shortages were a daily occurrence. The truck was half full, and I was sure things would be back to normal with tanker deliveries soon.

J didn't come up until Friday, mainly to save strain on the limited water supply. He brought a couple of gallons.

But my lessons didn't quit. Next day in the lesson, Celia told me to get Rocket's attention. She said, "She has yours, but I'd like you to try to get hers." I could tell we were entering a higher level of horsemanship. We were working on the intangible things. I didn't ask her how to get the horse's attention. I knew: You have to find the way yourself.

Reflections in the
Present Tense IV

It's an election year, Obama again or Romney, and it seems to me the pitch of the campaigning is just feverish. It is worse than the lead up to Christmas. Then, it's Election Day, Obama, and suddenly, it's all over, the news, the hype, the campaign. I mean, just like that. I have backlash. We are still recovering from Sandy, limbs are still down all over my place, and a nor'easter arrives at dusk on a Wednesday evening. I'm having fairly productive day, for me: paying bills, going to the gym. Exhausted all day. Wish they would bump my damn levothyroxine.

I have a thought . . . about the Thing. It's a breakdown of my coping mechanisms. Sometimes it's triggered by change. Sometimes, by other things, almost anything, it seems. And it's a real suspension of caring for myself. Sometimes I still feel I need to be punished, it seems, that I am a bad girl. It's connected to the idea that if only I suffer enough, it will stop.

But I think about how it feels when I'm taking care of my horse. How there is always a tenderness and a wonder about it.

I care so much for Chey. There is such a pleasant feeling, not just warmth, but light, in taking care of her, that it makes me wonder, why don't I have that same feeling about myself? Wouldn't it be nice if taking care of *me* gave me as much plea-sure as taking care of *her*. Why isn't it? Why isn't it pleasant to take care of myself? Do I feel I am not worth it? Why am I not worth it?

I think the answers to those questions will be important to address.

It's snowing, first snow of the season. Call me crazy, call me irresponsible, but I always love it when it snows. Predicting three to seven inches. Wow. As fast as the campaign leaves, the winter arrives.

Ch-ch-ch-changes

Something accelerated. We had refinanced the house in August. That winter, I talked to J about buying me out at the recently appraised value, plus the gutters we just had done. I must say we were being very civil during that time. And that's because I gave up. I starting thinking about moving on, but more seriously this time, apparently, because I found a house I could like in a good location for my horse, I had gotten pre-approved for a mortgage, I had asked Lance to run the numbers, and I had talked to J about the price at which he'd buy me out. It'd never gotten quite this far before, but I never felt so resigned to things as I was when that winter began.

I didn't know how to approach it. We were going up to Wassaic to ride the bikes to Millerton. He had gotten a sandwich at Subway, the Italian B.M.T. While we were in the car and he was eating his sandwich, I asked. He answered without much hesitation. He said, "Yeah, sure." Before, whenever we talked about it, he was all about how much profit he was aiming for (which would have required a price substantially over the recent appraisal). Now, he was ready to move quickly, more quickly than I was, anyway. I had mixed feelings. How can one not be hurt at the ease with which the person you thought of as a partner of some kind can embrace the idea of breaking up, when it's a little demanding for you?

Anyway, asked and answered, and I felt the need to ride my bike hard. For almost the entire ride, I so far in front that I couldn't even see him behind me anymore. I waited for him two or three times, but for the rest of it, I pumped rubber and rode on ahead . . . and stopped looking back.

It seems, oddly enough, that you don't start to see things clearly until you take a step back, let go of whatever emotional investment you have, and just observe. Like with the horse. You needed to stop thinking about how you feel. The horse doesn't care how you feel. Start thinking about the horse and what she's telling you. If you do, you make much better decisions about what to do next. I also realized something about J's eagerness to help me move on. It wasn't that he wanted me to go. It was that at every juncture, he felt he could help most by withdrawing. When he knew he was displeasing me, he retreated. This was his way of helping. I saw that and appreciated it. You needed to take the emotion out of it to see things clearly. And I found that house on Parliman I thought I'd like. So, things were moving ahead.

Not

It was a rocky time. When I called the realtor to go to the house on Parliman to take some measurements, she told me the house was no longer available, it was under contract.

This could have set me off on a binge, but I'd been acquiring some tools that helped. I began to see that having some structure in your life is important, because it helps automate the important things, like eating regularly and well. One of the things that always had accompanied a veer off the tracks is I started having trouble with food. Structure, like, the gym three times a week, and taking the time to prep appropriate things to eat during the day, taking care of your body, always accompanied a good time in my soul. I missed the gym today—just didn't feel like it. I didn't like my gym clothes, I didn't think they were flattering, and I didn't feel like attractive gym gear was a kosher expenditure. But I had Chey to center my days, and she always got me right.

It was the weekend after Thanksgiving 2012, Saturday afternoon. Chilly November day, gray, winds warning of cold. Got the first of my winter colds. Nyquil high. Worst was over, but still terribly congested and really out of it. I could sneak in a ride but didn't even want to try. Getting more realistic about the relationship between Chey and me. She didn't love me. She recognized me; that was all. She knew I was her human.

I had barely recovered when I had a lesson and I had such a bad ride with the Rocket that it colored my whole week. Depressed, sick, wondering what was worth it. I almost quit, was considering in my mind how I'd tell Celia and Donna that I didn't want to ride that horse anymore, that I was past my comfort zone. But I didn't. Next Wednesday, I went, at 9:30 a.m. up in Clinton (meant I had to get up by 6:00 a.m. to do my yoga stuff, like my balance and breathing stuff, and have a very hot bath and eat a considered breakfast and ONE cup of coffee only). And . . . it was the first real winter morning. We had a brief snow a couple of weeks before, before Hurricane Sandy. That was a fluke. This was the first real snow of the season beginning to come down. I was worried about a lot of things. Was I warmed up enough, well rested enough, well nourished enough, to try to ride that horse that day?

She was good. Not nearly as high, alert, concerned as my last ride, but of course, Donna had moved her operation about an hour north, and my ride last time on Rocket was Rocket's first exposure to the big indoor arena at this new place. Come to think of it, I could have eased my mind by remembering what Chey was like her first two weeks at Redmont. I didn't enjoy it much, but I didn't go off. And Celia didn't push me past where she felt I'd be safe. Told me that she was getting crazy because I was pushing her with my seat and pulling her with my hands. Which I was doing because she was moving so much and so fast

I was unable to catch my balance. Told me to back it off to a trot and call it a day.

After that, I had such a bad week emotionally and physically that I had to Nyquil my way through two nights. An anxiety nightmare about losing not only my truck, but my cell phone, and my cat Pippie, the new one. That was a lot of anxiety for one dream. I felt that I lost a week. And then my throat got fuzzy again, and worse after taking my next lesson, but the lesson was so worth it.

Rocket was her animated self, and while she was a handful, she was a handful I could hold. I didn't feel like loping her today, and Celia didn't make me. But today I could feel her again, all I felt last week was motion as she flung me around.

I had a major experience. Celia was blasé about having a bad day on a horse. And because she was blasé, it put one bad day in perspective. "You *make* it a good day, because you get something that you want out of it."

Jeez, is it as simple as that? Celia said that whatever day it is, a horse trainer may not like the horse he's riding, but he's got a job to do, and you get it done. Take the emotion out of it. Learn to address your fears more productively. Getting things done with horses is a kind of following through. Figure out what's preventing you from getting what you want from the horse. It is the figuring it out that makes you a better horseperson. Doing something about it makes you better, period. It's up to *you* to make it a good ride.

Recognize the experience and keep some distance from it. It need not overwhelm you; it can serve you. And it's not always your fault. Everyone has a day that could have gone better. I want to remind myself of all the days that did.

Rumination

I began been taking walks in the late afternoon. Snowy winter afternoons have such an appeal for me. When properly dressed, I love the urgency in the wind and the cold that pushes you to walk more vigorously, the stretch and use of muscles, the swinging of arms and legs, the looseness of motion. The light is wonderful at *l'heure bleue*, cloudy grays yielding to velvets. I love that time of day. It's a time of day and an activity that encourages rumination, and that is what I find on these walks.

Then I came home and came in through the garage that connected to J in his man-cave. He was watching football. It was such a jarring remove from the woods, the snow, and the night. A moment before, I had been standing in the backyard, searching for the Big Dipper and the other constellations I know, and thinking that the ancient Greeks, who named them, saw them just as I did, although from a little further south. Then, booey! The Game. All inspiration evaporated in the dancing colors and shapes on the tube, transfixing me almost totally. And I had an interesting thought.

Wouldn't it be something if I found more meaning in my life without this relationship as it is than I do with it? If it were actually not only not contributing anything to my emotional well-being, but detracting from it?

Hmmm.

Letting go of the idea that J and I were one thing, when we were clearly something else. We were meant to be pals, doing things together, holidays, vacations, backup. With any luck, it'll be that way again, like it was before we bought the house together. The house was a mistake. Our friendship wasn't.

Rose-Colored Glasses

I had been so happy to have a horse, and especially, to have this horse. The two I had before were enough to teach me that not every horse is something you dream about. This one was, to the ten-year old girl I became almost the moment Chey walked into my life.

But . . . to someone who knows horses, she isn't much. She isn't young. She isn't built well. Her hindquarters are small, which means no engine, no power. She is front heavy and pulls herself along, instead of pushing herself from behind as she should. As a result, she overstresses her front legs, and since I've had her, she has torn a tendon in each. She can't collect easily because her anatomy doesn't encourage it. She has oddly long lips. She has extremely large feet.

But . . . I adore her. She is beautiful to me, half a ton of strawberry blonde, warm and fragrant. To stroke her, to put my arms around her neck and smell her, is a great joy to me.

It pisses Celia off no end. "She's not a pet. Quit hugging her and let's get going," she'll say in her "I mean business" voice.

And I just kept thinking about treating my horse like a pet, or like a horse. And then, I realized. Pets live in your house, in your life, they sleep in your bed. We find them endearing to the degree they act like us. Horses are different. If you want to interact with horses, you have to do it on their terms, on their turf, literally. And to value horses only to the degree they mimic human characteristics or emotions, is doing a disservice to horses.

It does a disservice to anyone, to value them only to the degree they resemble *you*. I was thinking about my relationship with J. He was a good guy—we'd been kind of together since 1991. So there was something there. Perhaps it just wasn't what I thought it was, what I assumed it was, after buying the house together, and all. Perhaps I was reading this wrong, and that's why there was friction between us.

Baptism

Had a major blowout with J. We were invited to the baptism of his nephew's first son. He knows I am not religious, and not of *his* religion, and was wildly afraid I would say or do something inappropriate. I tried to make a joke about it, but it hit him wrong, and he demanded I get out of the car and not go into the church. I said his nephew had invited me, too, and I was going. That set off a very unpleasant time for us.

What a change a day can bring.

I was still riding other horses in my lessons. I went up to Donna's after I did my stint at the pony farm, looking forward to riding Mikky because that was always better than riding Rocket. When I got there, Donna said to me, "We've been having a lot of fun with Rocket." Well, good for you. Donna has started horses[5] and runs the barn, and her daughter, Gillian,

---

5. In the bad old days, the term used was to "break" a horse. Today, the term "start" a horse is preferred.

is sixteen and has grown up with horses. Of course they are having fun. Running and bucking and jumping are fun for them. I wondered why she was telling me this.

I got out Mikky's tack and grooming tools. I found Celia in the office and chirped happily, "I'm riding Mikky?" "No," she said. "Rocket."

WHAT?!?!. Huh no, like I really need this right now. My face must have fallen a yard. Mikky has an issue in his left rear leg. He's off. Can't ride him. I know I can trust Celia . . . but . . .

So I went and got Rocket. She did not come to me like she usually would, we had about six inches of combined snow and frozen sleet on the ground, and I was wearing my new cowboy boots, which have absolutely no traction, so I slipped and slid and limped across the paddock to get Rocket and slipped and slid and limped all the way back, tugging on Rocket to make her stop leading me while trying to not fall down. She was a little nervous. Celia saddled her while I put away the stuff I would have used on Mikky, and I took her into the big indoor to lunge her. Rocket took off like her tail was on fire, threw a few bucks, and settled down into a run. I got her down to a trot, turned her, and off we went in the other direction. Then, I brought her in, bridled her, and with Celia holding her, got on and just sat there, my mind trying to find a still place.

Off we went in the jog, and something was different. I was sitting back, hands low, riding with my legs, like I had learned on Mikky. She was not fighting the bit; she was not punting to go into a run. "Keep her at the speed *you* want," said Celia. To my amazement, I could.

We jogged over the ground poles, over the cross rail, circles, spirals, lines, stops. She was a different horse. I was *enjoying* riding her. I felt connected to her. I felt her. I could feel her body, getting to feel when she bowed out, starting to feel when she's on her front end versus her hind end. I don't know why it has taken four years for me to learn to feel the horse, but whatever, it has and I'm starting. Occasionally, I'd would make a mistake—didn't catch her dropping her shoulder, or bowing out—and Celia would say, "Do you know what just happened there?" Not always—but sometimes I could tell. And I figured something out. If it's not working, don't get mad, don't get depressed. Just try something else.

It turns out that riding Rocket that day, that well, was *exactly* what I needed.

A Cold Winter

I had been really pissed at J after the baptism thing. So pissed I just didn't want to have anything to do with him. Answered when spoken to as briefly as possible. Made my own plans instead of waiting on him to tell me what we were doing that weekend. Working some things out in my head about what I want out of this. Waking up a little more to who he really is and what he wants from me. It's only a good thing, because, as it is with horses, you more you know about who he is, what he wants, the better you get at getting what *you* want out of the situation. Horse or human.

I was so angry that my fear of conflict began to recede. I decided that things were going to be different. I owned half this house, and I had rights, too. And if he didn't want to be part of my life, I was not going to force him. I was beginning to think I could handle that.

That weekend, I filled the wood cradles and had a fire going when he came up. I could tell he knew he was in the doghouse.

I had had my dinner. I had turned the oven on for him when I heard the garage door, and when he came up, I said so. Then I left. He put away his groceries and put his pizza in the oven. At some point, I came back and said, "You notice I got a fire going and filled up the wood cradles? "Yes," he said. "It would be good if you could do the same some time over the weekend." "Yes, yes," he said, instead of giving me the argument I expected.

Then we'd usually watch a movie on TV (he had gotten Dish for the house so he could watch the games). He suggested a few. I agreed to watch *The Adventures of Tintin*. Then I left to go to bed without announcing it, blew out the candles, and asked, "Would you check the fire before you go to sleep?" "Yes, yes," he responded. Good.

Next day, I got a call from Katy from the barn. Her sister and a friend came over on a whim and they'd all be at the barn for a couple of hours if I'd like to come and play. "Sure!" I said, and then told J, "I'm going to go to the transfer station, and then I'm going to go play at the barn for a few hours. When I come back, I'll haul up some wood, which would be easier if you could move your car." "OK, good."

In the meantime, he vacuumed, putting the dining room chairs on top of the table. He organized some of the garbage and brought some down to the big can in the garage. He was changing tablecloths, and it looked like he dusted a little. When he moved the candle I had in the hall, I said, "So I can't have my candle there anymore?" and he said, "No, I'm just cleaning the table." All in all . . . a very satisfactory day so far.

After the barn, with Katy, her sister, and a friend, we went to Daily Planet, and at some point, Karen offered a toast, "May we all accept ourselves unconditionally just as we are." It struck me what a wonderful thing that would be. And after the last few days, having had it with J, I thought maybe I was getting there—maybe I was beginning to like myself a little bit. I couldn't have been feeling that way if I wasn't.

I had such a lovely moment with Chey the day before. She seemed to have become very much more responsive in the last few days after a period of not paying much attention to me. I didn't think I could ride her because of the cold and the footing, so after I fed and groomed her, I turned her back out and spent some time with her. We were standing by the round bale feeder, and she was nibbling like a horse who was not really hungry, just picking, her eyes half closed. She was so sweet. I began to pull out some tufts of hay through the nibble net and gave them to her. She waited politely for me to offer and took each morsel with care not to pinch my fingers. I stopped pulling out tufts. She finished the one she had and ever so gently touched my arm with her muzzle as if to say, *May I have another, please?* It was just so sweet. I wanted to show her that I was smart, too, and I could learn a cue. So I fed her a few more times when she asked and then told her to feed herself. What a lovely interlude. What a lovely Chey.

Little Successes

Little Successes. Horses teach us about realistic expectations.

The little steps I took with Chey were like the beads on a necklace, and every bead was a positive moment. I was not just anybody to this horse. She stops when I do instead of shoving ahead ignoring me. There's a bead. She willingly picks up her feet so I can clean them. Bead. Drops her head to be bridled. Bead. Waits until told to move. Bead.

My childhood, and the life that followed, convinced me that I was all but worthless. But this horse didn't think so. She paid attention to me, obeyed me, and little by little, was coming to trust me. This thousand-pound animal was willing to do what I asked. This horse brought me entirely into the present moment. My world was changing because of it.

Donna said that I could come up and ride Rocket any time I wanted, even if Celia wasn't there. I would pay a small fee for the use of the place, as was customary. One day, I decided to do it. The weather was threatening, dark, cold, but I was not going to back down. I got to her barn, said, "Hi, thought I'd ride Rocket today!" and with Donna's nod I went to get her. Saddled her, lunged her, bridled her, and got on. I sat soft, light hands, soft eyes, breathed, and we walked and trotted around the ring, small circles, bigger circles, over ground poles, between barrels, and I wrapped it up with a little lope around the arena in one direction and a lope around the arena in the other. Thunder started rolling over the tin roof, and I kept working the horse, thinking about what I wanted her to do, and we kept on working. We had a good ride.

2013

Another new year was under way. I wondered how it would be different and how the same.

I had the idea of a creative space, but not in your house, in your mind. Describing it seemed so mundane in comparison to what it really felt like, that really nice feeling I had when I was feeling creative. I wished I could catalog and dissect it, so that I could recall it when I wanted it, and fend off the destructive tides that seemed always to be present.

"I accept myself unconditionally, just as I am."

Katy's sister had said, keep saying it out loud. Why is that so hard for me?

"I accept myself unconditionally, just as I am."

There must be something to it. Everything I've learned about the Way—from *The Tibetan Book of Living and Dying*, *Zen and the Art of Motorcycle Maintence*, Deepak Chopra, or Chey— points to it. So if it would help, I would do it. Could I say it, at least, for now, in my mind, every day as soon as I was conscious. I wondered if I could change my paradigm. I'd bet I could.

Rode Cloudy on Tuesday at Jason's, turning back for Celia, and felt the way he moved, and suddenly, finally, I understood. It was time to get another horse.

How very strange to feel this way about the horse who brought me back, but I saw now what it was about. It was about seeing and accepting what is. I wanted to get better, and Celia kept telling me, the only way I could get better was to ride better horses. Chey was wonderful at what she did, but I wanted to do more. It wouldn't be fair to ask or expect her to. I didn't love her any the less. I would take care of her for the rest of her life. But I saw one way I could do more stuff, and at that time, it was turning back for Celia with Cloudy.

Chey knew it, too. After working with Celia at her place and at Jason's, I went to see Chey about 2:30 p.m. When she saw I didn't have a halter and I didn't have a bucket, she looked at me politely and went back to her grass. This horse had been the center of my world for so long and I loved her—and I was ready to give her a brother.

Cycles

I see the cycles, I guess. The periods where I am writing are periods when I feel good about me and about being me. The other more manic times, are when I don't. I had a lesson with Celia one Friday and we were doing some rollbacks on Cloudy. I was in a hurry to get it right. "You don't have to rush" she smiled. Oh? Really?

Despite being five years from my ferocious life in finance, I still had periods where I felt myself rushing, being driven by some great imperative, about what I didn't know, but the drive was irresistible . . . But I came to realize at least, that that is a stage, it doesn't have to be who I am. I think not rushing is a clue to something that would help move me toward something more positive in my emotional life.

Don't rush. Be in this moment, not the next one.

I accept myself unconditionally, just as I am.

I think these two are related.

J and I truly were living apart together. We were both people afraid of too much inspection. We were both very uncomfortable with conflict. But that was what's held us together, I thought. We were held together as much by our common fears as by our common interests. But I found that when I stopped thinking about what he "lacked," and started thinking about why he did what he did—and it was not that you have no feelings about it exactly, you were doing it because you cared—things went better between us. When you took the emotion out of it, you could see things more clearly, because only then could you see them for what they really were. I found out with the horses, you didn't have to get invested in every interaction, you just had to pay attention and try to learn. You didn't have to rush. You didn't have to be afraid of failing. Or falling. You could let it go. When you let that go, it was no longer failure. It was just something that didn't work. So, you tried something else.

I could let it go and exist totally in the moment. Like horses do. The total *now* of the natural world. It used to be I couldn't get there without some substance to help—alcohol, tobacco, whatever. Now, I just needed Chey. When you were in the now, you could observe without judgment. You could participate without fear. You could let it go.

The force that made me do these things that were unproductive at best, destructive at worst, was a negative thing. The things that took me in the opposite direction: Chey, honest exercise, outdoor hikes with J in all seasons, friends, the writing workshops, the cats. Things that were not good for me: alcohol, tobacco, sugar, television. When I came into contact with those things, I needed to be particularly careful. When Sting glowed blue . . .

Turning Sixty

It's if I could keep myself focused on horses, writing, and friends, I was at my best. When my focus drifted to negative things—like the things I used to think I should have done, or who I thought I should have been and how I failed—when I thought about the shortcomings of other people, things went bad with me, which was bad for everything else, because you can't get good from bad.

So if I could stay focused on those things, I could be healthier. I thought that was worth the effort, especially now that things were proving so positive for me. Celia's birthday card to me said: "In a heaven full of stars, there are always some that burn a little brighter . . . like you." That's what I can be if I can hold on to the good things, of which there are so many more, these days.

In spring 2013, I blew my back out again. Didn't know what I did. But I did know that when I was off routine, off exercise and careful food, and off Chey, things got screwed up.

I'd been thinking about the riding I did for Celia as a turn-back rider. She had hooked me up with Jason's horse, and he was letting me ride him for nothing, which was generous of him. Usually, if you rode someone else's horse, or used their ring, you paid them something. I should have been giving him something for the use of Cloudy. Cloudy was a good little horse, built well, athletic. He was born on a ranch out West, lived on the range until he was old enough to get started. I'd been riding him all season. And I realized, if I wanted to keep doing this for Celia, I really needed a horse who could do the job. She'd been telling me for two years that it was time to move on. It occurred to me . . . Cloudy might be the horse! Then, since he trailered so well, handled cows so well, maybe I could take the next step and actually work at this. I needed to think about this.

Chey was relaxing in the sun as I went to her the next day. We had the remains of a foot of snow that had fallen the night before, melting so successfully by the fifty-degree day that by then it was just scuffs. She turned her head when I opened the gate, but seemed in a reverie, and it took a moment for me to register. She nickered at the pink bucket I was carrying and came over. And she stayed, after the meal, and we fooled around a little, me trying to find places she wanted scratched, and she encircling me with her head and neck, which I think was "horse" for a hug. My back was still very delicate, after another emergency room trip earlier in the week. But it was a lovely day with her.

Then, there was the "cardiac" event. I was still on thyroid medicine, but since what I was taking didn't really leave me feeling very awake, my doctor and I had just added another medication that approached the problem a little differently at a very low dose to try. I was on both of the medications when Celia gave a clinic at Jason's place for five or six people who wanted to get better at cutting. I was there to help in any way I could. It was a cold day, and despite all the horses and people in the arena, I was freezing. The only thing hot to drink was some coffee Jason provided, but as the day wore on, it got very, very strong. I tried not to drink too much, but I was so cold.

That night, about 10:00 p.m., my heart started racing and pounding with alarming force and irregularity. I could barely breathe, and my whole body vibrated with the pulse. J took me to the Emergency Room, and I was admitted as a cardiac patient. How adult. I had filled out the forms, and they had me on a gurney when the attending physician came to interview me and review my chart. "Are you or do you think you might be pregnant?" he said. Scared as I was I guffawed. "I'm sixty years old!" I said. "Well, you look very young," the doctor rejoined a little sheepishly.

The old thyroid medicine plus the new thyroid medicine plus a little too much caffeine had put my heart into atrial fibrillation, an "a-fib." I found I really didn't like being in the hospital, handing my body over to so many strangers, even though all of them were wonderful. I was handled by about a dozen people, all doing their jobs, and I could see this would be a difficult job to do if you didn't like doing it; because, that's what it was like for me, that all these people were genuinely interested in helping me through this. My second trip to the emergency room (it was my back last time) in as many weeks shook me. I knocked off the new medication and cut out caffeine almost entirely.

That event, my disappointment in my riding, and the unsteady state of having agreed to split up with J but having no place to go generated sufficient stress to put me in a danger zone, where I began to feel it was not worth it. Then my back went out, as it does periodically, and I was ready to call it quits. When I realized that was what I was thinking, I decided I needed to call E, a therapist a friend recommended, whom I had seen about three times in the last couple of years. He was wonderful, and had given me some real tools to cope. Just making the decision to call him—and taking the step to help myself solve a problem positively—had already made me feel a little better.

He seemed to remember me precisely. Everything. He asked about how that relationship thing was going. I said we had decided the house thing wasn't working. I'd looked at houses for the last two springs and just never found anything that really appealed to me. I told him I was scared of being on my own. E nodded.

He said my problem was not self-esteem, but anxiety, which stemmed from a distorted view of what I had control over in my life, and what I didn't. He said it was like the right rearview mirror on your car. The view behind was distorted. And that it might help to realize, that the greater the anxiety I faced, the less likely it was to be connected to anything real. *Hmmm.*

After weeks of my back being too tender to test, I finally got back on a horse again, West. He belonged to Donna and was a "finished" horse, meaning trained to the max. He was a Haflinger, a heavy horse, and a doll. It was a group lesson. Celia spoke mostly to Bobbie, which I guess meant that I was doing OK. I guessed. I did get the correct lead on him. It felt like his right front was picking up higher. I always figured it would be his left rear I'd feel. I was looking for the wrong thing, so I hadn't felt the right thing when it happened. Until that day.

I was feeling depressed. My financial adviser gave me the go-ahead to get another horse under the parameters I described. Providing we continued to earn 5 percent on the portfolio. I fully understood what it meant, when the model showed it worked. How could I not? I spent eighteen years futzing models so they would work, but I didn't think my adviser did that. Still, no one can know the future. And . . . now, I'd be handling a house on my own. We hadn't accounted for that.

My first impulse when I felt like that was to get high on something and watch a movie, to get drunk or eat a pie. I wanted to see if I could get by that day without any of the above. I went to feed Chey and spent some time in the field with her. And that day, I could.

Spring 2013

I was lonely for a Passover seder. Family was spread all over the country by now. I had made several seders at my little apartment, taking the baton from Mom when she was in her eighties. I tried to do one up at the house, but turns out I was the only Jew in attendance. In fact, a friend I'd invited came with a book. "I don't know what your Bible is, but this is mine," she said. She held it out to me: *Judaism for Dummies*. I hooted.

I knew I'd be welcome at a local synagogue and went to a reform seder at Temple Beth Elohim. Reform enough that it opened with a musical number, "There's *no* seder like *our* seder, like *no* seder I *know* . . ." It was a very nice experience, and good to be in the company of people with the same memories and traditions I was brought up with. Called J to check that he'd got the message from his sister about his neighbor. His neighbor Johnny, a friend from childhood, who was a little younger than J, died that day of a heart attack. He did, and we talked about that for a while. And it struck me: We actually talked about something. And J even allowed as how it was kind of shocking, on a lot of levels. Intimations of mortality.

And then, to my amazement, he listened about the seder, and made a joke about how reform it was. And then, get this: He asked me what I wore to it.

Something was happening here. It was comforting, whatever it was, and pleasant.

Working It

I got to the gym. I talked to E. Here are the tools he shared with me:

1. Part of anxiety is having a distorted rearview that says you are responsible for more than you actually are. Random chance makes up so much of who we turn out to be.
2. Part of anxiety is like a car alarm that goes off when the garbage truck passes. All kinds of things can set it off, but not all of them are legit.
3. The worse the anxiety gets, the less likely it is attached to anything real, i.e., the worse it is, the more likely it's false.
4. There is no moral superiority because someone is better than you at something. It's just the breaks. Their talents are morally neutral.

Then I rode Chey, and she was back to her old good self, and then Francie the equine masseuse came to give her a massage.

Francie saw something very special in Chey, and Chey knew Francie was someone she could trust, and within moments Chey was grooming me as vigorously as Francie was massaging her. It really did my heart good to see Chey enjoying it so, to be able to do something that nice for her. And Francie was so pleasant, and she made my horse feel so good, it was a wonderful afternoon of love and Chey.

Cowboying

I love working holding cows for Celia. The best thing to do on horseback is a job, and the best job to do on horseback is cows. I decided the time had come. I couldn't keep riding Cloudy for nothing. And if I wanted to do this job, I needed a horse who could do it. I told Celia and Jason that I'd like to buy the horse. Big smiles all around. Jason and I shook on it and agreed to payment terms. I'd pay Celia her fee when I gave Jason the down payment. She gave me a great big smile and hugged me hard.

Wow.

I really never thought I'd have a chance to cowboy again, outside of Wyoming. But here I was, in a construction site in Connecticut, cowboying for Celia. It was a dream. No, not really a dream. Once it was a dream, but now, it was what I was doing, pursuing horsemanship, working with horses, doing a real job on horseback. It seemed it couldn't be true. It scared me that it was true, because how much would I have to pay someday for this happiness, because happiness had been so elusive for me, at any price, and now it was here. . . . There was still a part of me that didn't believe I deserved this. Talking about my life with Celia at dinner with friends one day, reminded me of how sad and lonely so much of it was, but I wanted to just leave that alone where it was, in the past, and move wholeheartedly into today. I wouldn't be punished for being happy anymore.

I told J how excited I was to be riding for real, for a job, and that I was going to buy Cloudy, who'd stay in Connecticut for the summer season and come back to Redmont for the winter. He said that he could see this was something I wanted to do, and I had to live my life, but if I got another horse, he really didn't want to share the house with me anymore.

Pause. There it was. In black-and-white. It had come and it was now.

"Would you let me buy you out at current market value?" I asked. "Yes," he said. And I realized in a flash I could not afford to buy Cloudy. I was disappointed—but not crushed. I still had Chey. The time will come. In fact, perhaps all for the best. Buying J out, splitting up, will be change enough to cope with, and I had become kinder to myself when it came to things like this. And, I was to see there was still plenty I could do with Cheyenne. We had not nearly exhausted the possibilities.

So I went through the mortgage application process, he was being reasonable, and I was so right about something. It's always better to go for something you love, than run from something you don't. And I was right. It *is* always better to go toward something than away from something. I hadn't found any house I liked as much as this one; I knew it, what to expect, what needed doing. I loved this little house. It was going to be OK. I began to feel so good about things. I had a horse I loved, and I had a gig with Celia.

And because I have found my "something better," changing the relationship with J assumed its appropriate importance in my life: It was an experiment that didn't work out, but one that forced me to learn a lot. I was just considering this a change in living arrangements. There should be no reason two people who feel that doing this is the best thing for both of them can't move through this as friends. That turned out to be true. We were much better friends before we started sharing the house. That was the right relationship for us. We became much better friends afterward, too.

I had a wonderful ride with Chey that day. She had just had her seasonal massage, so Francie cautioned she might be a little sore, but she didn't seem so at all and was much more game than I would have thought. I still took it easy on her. Just about half an hour of light work, a little loping, and then grass on the halter. I was trying to pay particular attention to her body, to feel through her if there was anything wrong, stiff, sore. I hoped I would learn to read that, about her. I admitted it. I loved her. There was a place in me that was so excited to be moving through this time, riding better horses, getting more and more comfortable, more confident; riding seriously, with a purpose, every day; but there was also a place in me which was a ten-year old girl with her first pony. That was me and Chey, and I realized that was so important to me, too. And I could have both. I was multitudes.

J was visiting family in Florida, the first trip we had not taken together since we met in 1991. And I was having a taste of what life without him as a roommate would be. He gave my week punctuation, coming up Friday nights. Guess I would have to figure out another way to do that.

At this point, it looked like I would not be able to keep two horses. And even if I could, it would be wrong for me to neglect my beloved Chey while pursuing cowboy work with Cloudy. Although Chey did not have the build to do the kind of work Cloudy could, she still had developed substantial skills and strength in the five years we'd been together. She was about the best trail horse you could hope for—level, careful, kind. Spooked at almost nothing. Would go over, under, around or through, anything. Would not race toward home. It would be a pity to waste that. And as I discovered at the rescue place where I volunteered, horses are a lot like people in one regard. If they stay active and engaged, they remain healthier, mentally and physically, than horses/people who don't. So, even if I was able to keep both Chey and Cloudy, I had begun to consider: If I could find the right home for Chey, near enough that I could still see her from time to time, where she would be loved and appreciated as much as I loved and appreciated her, I'd think about it.

A possibility emerged. It would be a woman who would keep her at home, ride her gently, keep her forever as she had her other horses that were now too old to ride. Nearby, so I could still see her. Recommended by two people, including Susie, who had never steered me wrong. Now, I knew that once I gave up Shammes, my life went on quite well, but Chey meant so much to me, and what with changing the living arrangements, I was not sure about making too many changes at once. And frankly, I think she is so beautiful, I am proud to ride her. Cloudy is cute, but he hasn't got her style.

Celia would say, "Take the emotion out of it." But I don't want to, in this case. Horses are not a job, they are a love, and at this moment, I'm not ready to give up my anchor, my beautiful Chey. I did not call the lady back.

On the other front: Celia said I was now her "crew." That season, she hadn't the money to compete, so the deal at Jason's would be short-lived, but I would still help her out at her place,

loping, cooling, showering off, etc., three or four hours if we
didn't go to Jason's, six or so if we did. And, I continued taking
lessons from Celia, for which I was paying full price. I knew she
wouldn't be sympathetic to my feelings about Chey. She wanted
me to buy Cloudy.

Morning at the pony farm. Rainy afternoon at home, some
e-mails and phone calls between the mortgage broker, financial
adviser, and me. The mortgage broker asked me every time if I
had any debt. They were having a hard time reconciling my
income with my tax returns, as I told them they would and are
looking for evidence that I had repaid something recently. I
realized I should have refinanced that truck. Maybe the mortgage was not so sure as all that.

Around 6:30 p.m., I decided to take a walk in the rain, my
usual stroll up the Mount Tom road to the top, and back. J had
come up, and was later arriving than I expected and I found
myself getting irritated at him, and decided that the best way to
make lemonade out of that lemon of a thought was to take a
walk.

When I came back, I saw his car was indeed in the garage.
But it was such a pleasant spring rain, mild thunder in the distance reassuring you it was warm (although thunder in January,
as we had had in the last two years, is an ominous sign of the
dissolution of that association) and rainy days are the absolute
best for weeding, so I did some work on the parking rail "garden." Maybe I could do something nicer with it.

As my hands became stained with dirt, I thought. It occurred
to me that caring about something creates the energy to achieve
it. This little piece of Planet Earth might become mine. And if
I let myself, I might let go and allow myself to feel something.
Commitment. I was always scared about commitment—felt I
couldn't trust my judgment—but, I found that as I engaged in

those things I have committed to, I sought escape less. Working in my little garden in the rain, I thought I came to a new understanding of what that meant. For me, it meant you'd rather do it than watch television. For me, television was mindless escape, my response to stress. But these days, the less time I spent in front of screens, the better my life went. The less stressed I was, the more engaged I was in my life. And the more engaged I was in my life, the less stressed I was.

Chapter . . . Four

Trailered the horses Sunday to the cell tower ride, just wonderful. Lesson on Zip. Felt something. Felt the ground. Really important lesson today. Couldn't get it on Chey.

I was inspired by Louise and her sister's enthusiasm to go for that other thing I wanted, which was, to *show*. We needed to be sharp and light, because if Louise and Vera's super grooming prep, the clipping, the bathing, the conditioning, the combing, the slinkies on their manes and tails count for a lot, we were not going to be in the competition. They had fancier horses, too. But perhaps, Chey and I communicated well enough to give them a run for it, so I was being more demanding, I was riding with a purpose again, like I did when I first started this life.

So . . . we worked every day in the ring. And I realized that we needed more work on trailering, which involved another off-site expedition with the horses. Wethersfield. What a wonderful day with Chey, and a whole gang from the barn at that astonishingly beautiful estate with miles of dedicated bridle trails. It was like the queen's estate at Balmoral. Chey was getting so much better every time, and I believed she was happy when she was on a new trail. She was obedient and cooperative when we did exercises in the ring, but it was on the trail she really excelled.

We came to a jump, which was a fallen log; while others were thinking about jumping it, she gamely walked over it, like, *Hey, I got this!* I didn't want to push her, after the torn tendon. And then, as we were going along, we came to some low jumps. She was into it, so I gave her the go-ahead, and she sailed over the two jumps as proud as punch.

After the ride, we sponged off the horses and let them eat some grass, and put them back in the horse trailer. It was the first time I had ever asked Chey to just hang out in there while we ate lunch. She did calmly. I thought, *This is wonderful, so many vistas open up for me with a truck, a horse trailer, and a horse who will trailer comfortably.*

Then, as the summer show season began, another glorious day, working cows on horseback at Celia's and then working cows on horseback over at Jason's. I got to ride Zip and Cloudy. Dirty, sweaty, sandy. This was not what I was I was hoping for; this was so much better than anything I hoped for; better than anything I could have imagined for in the old days, in the days of my life until horses. Admittedly, I was in some pain: I was riding fast horses making sharp turns four to six hours a day. Celia would not let me post. I had to sit every maneuver. I would get blisters on the skin over my sit bones. And it was a hundred degrees. The blisters went beyond ruptured to chewed. Pantyhose are recommended to prevent blisters. Bike shorts, too. It was too late for prevention, but I tried them anyway— salve, bandages, pantyhose, and bike shorts under my jeans. One day, I was wearing this getup as we worked at Celia'a and then

Jason's. When we got in her car to come home from Jason's, the thermometer read 104 degrees. How I avoided passing out from heat stroke, I don't know.

I was happy. Yes, this is what it felt like.

Celia's husband, Kyle, was taking a shine to me. He was quite a bit older than Celia, a second- or third-generation horse trader. He began to take a role in my education. Yesterday, he had me lope Zip around a bit after we finished with the cows. And . . . a remarkable thing. He told me about a time he went to work with a big name in reining, expecting he'd be doings spins and sliding stops. "You can't even lope a horse in a circle!" he was told. And he devoted the whole workshop just learning how to lope a horse in a circle. He used to spend a lot of time barking at me, but this was the first time he ever said anything encouraging. I felt it marked a milestone in our relationship. Celia thought so, too. Then, I heard he told Celia, "Looks like she's learning how to sit on a horse." I must have been doing OK.

The House

I was feeling good: I gave up on the mortgage broker and just went to the bank we already had the mortgage with. They were fine with me continuing alone. The bank's appraiser came; J's came. It was moving ahead. I was really feeling there was more to be gained than lost in this. And I wasn't losing as much as I thought, because I never had it, actually, so it was not really a loss.

From the beginning, J had no problem assuming ownership of stuff; space, Tupperware, whatever. For example, one day he put some Klondike bars in "my" section of the freezer, which was already less than half his. I mentioned it, and he said testily, "I ran out of room." "Yeah," I said, "I know. You need to thin down your freezer compartment."

Well, today, *I* ran out of room. So I put a few things in "his" area. I was claiming my space.

Transitions

We went on a group trail ride; it was my first experience at Steep Rock. What a wonderful day with my horse and others. I thought of all the things that were new to me such a short time ago, and now were part of my life; driving the trailer, taking my horse places. Turning back. Getting ready to show. So many new things. And . . . J leaving. So many new things, and I was not afraid. It seemed I was no longer as afraid as I had been my whole life to date. There was surely tension, but the paralyzing, all consuming anxiety in which I spent so much time was not there.

Then . . . I came home after this wonderful day to find that Jerry, my aging outdoor cat, my little terror, was dead. I didn't want to put it in print. I wasn't ready for it. He was old, it was true, and one is never ready for it, but still. He was the last cat I got as a kitten. It was back in 1993, I had just lost Sheriff Parsley; and it was J who hooked me up with the colleague who found Jerry, abandoned in the hallway of a New York City apartment building in a box with some kibble. I didn't think I was ready for another cat at the time, but Jerry jumped right up on the ottoman and touched noses. It didn't take long to see he was born to be wild, so we brought him up to the country, where he was master of all he surveyed. I cut a cat door in the garage. He'd sashay around the property like a little lion, and kept the house and garage free from rodents of all kinds. I finally had a life I wanted; so I knew how happy he was to be up here. I wished he hadn't died; it would have been nice to have him keeping me company on the property, following me around when I did the outside chores, once the house was mine.

I was glad we buried him there; he was so happy up at the house. And maybe his ghost would visit me, if I let it. Good ol' Jerry. The wacky guy. I would be OK with it if *my* eulogy contained no more than that I did right by him. Good ol' Jerry. Thanks for being in my life.

Time was flying by.

Yesterday, we were working cows at Celia and Kyle's, and I was riding Zip and leading Mr. P (one of the cutting horses) back after he worked. Five cows were in the big field we passed through. When I was at the gate, I got off, slipped the reins over Zip's neck, and slipped off his bridle, planning to put his halter on there instead of on the other side of the gate, so as not to lead him in wearing the bridle. His nose was in the halter and suddenly he exploded backward like he saw a rhino. I grabbed the reins around his neck, but he blasted off, pulled me onto my face in the dirt, still holding on to the other horse, but when I lost my footing, I let go of Zip. He went flying toward the arena and the cows, and I jumped up, still holding Mr. P, wondering what happened. "Are you all right!" cried Celia. "Yes, I'm fine," I said. No harm done. Two square inches of epidermis rasped off my left forearm, banged my hip, but I wasn't even feeling it.

I wasn't frightened, just so surprised at old, dead broke Zip exploding like that.

Poor Celia, put a few more gray hairs on her head.

Back home that night, I noticed something. It always seemed to me that it was mainly old people who displayed photographs. I've become old then, because I noticed that my room is filled with the pictures of those who have been important to me. And I noticed how few of those photographs were of people. Parsley, Goody, Jerry, Odin, Shammes, Chey; only Mom and Dad for people. And how many pictures I had of Chey, more than any other animal I've had. I wondered what this said about me. I was not worried, though.

The Show

By now, August 2013, Chey and I had been getting along pretty
well. I trusted her, and she trusted me. We had been going on
remote trail rides, and she loaded decent, traveled well, and kept
her head when we unloaded in a strange place. I could saddle
and bridle her without worrying about losing my horse. She
had been handling strange horses well; she excelled at obstacles
like mud, brush, jumps, and water. Last trail ride, six people
and their horses went along. There was a tunnel that was so
long and dark you *could not see the exit* until you were almost
upon it. Total blackness. Chey got a little snorty in that one and
kept asking me, *Are you sure you want to do this?* but we got
through it. What a brave horse. Then the friend who was kind
of a point person asked me to ride away from the group to see
if a certain trail branched off. I thought Chey was perhaps the
only horse in that group who would ride away from her herd in
a strange place without complaint. My good girl.

In addition to riding trails off the property, Louise, the

owner, and her sister, Victoria, hit just about every local horse show during the season. They went to the local shows run by groups like the Southern Dutchess Horse and Pony Association, the Woodstock Riding and Driving Club, and G&M, which used the Thomas Bull Memorial Park in Montgomery, New York, as their show grounds. These groups organized English and western shows for amateurs and open (amateur or pro) riders. Louise and Victoria, were avid show women. Artemis (we called her Artie) and Jill frequently joined them. Several times during the season, you would see them hauling out the show tack, saddles and bridles resplendent in silver and rawhide, ferrules and braiding, which they spent hours cleaning and polishing. Literally. Then, the horses would be brought in, and there would be a carnival of grooming, shampooing, conditioning, clipping, sanding, hoof polishing, banding, and wrapping their horses in slinky things to keep their manes clean and smooth. The truck and trailer would be hitched and pulled to the barn entrance; it would be loaded with tack, hay, water, show clothes, extra halters, and lead lines, Show Sheen, Leather New, first-aid kit, manure fork, lunch. The next day, by the crack of dawn, the gals and their horses would be off.

When they would return many hours later, they would be tired, sweaty, and happy. Louise would always win something, usually firsts or seconds. Grand Champion and Reserve Champion of her division pretty frequently. The others would also come home heavy, and it would just seem like a wonderful time.

"Gee. I think *I'd* like to show!" I said after they returned from a show in mid-August. "There's one coming up right down the road September 29," Louise responded, winking at me. She had been so very encouraging as she watched Chey and me play in the ring. "You're ready!"

Well . . . I decided to go for it! It was about six weeks away. I figured that would give me enough time to get my head right. I didn't even know what the events were, whether they measure horse or human or both, where do you sign up, how does it work? Louise took me in hand, showed me the booklet that described the classes and requirements, filled out my application, highlighted the information that would be relevant to me, and told me what division to enter. It would be Green Horse, because Chey and I had never shown before. Green Horse required less than two seasons in the show circuit. Technically, I could have entered the "Novice" division events as well, which would include riders who were just starting to lope in the show ring. Celia advised me against it. "If you ride in 'Novice,' you're going to get a lot of blowback." By which I took it to mean that I ride a little better than the typical "novice." First I heard of it; usually all Celia ever did was bang on me.

I entered in the five Green Horse division classes: Showmanship (a halter class to show an impeccably groomed, obedient, willing horse through several ground maneuvers); Road Hack, to show control of a calm, collected horse and rider at speed; Equitation, where the rider is judged; Western Pleasure, to show a relaxed, easy, pleasant-looking horse/rider combo in the walk, trot, and canter; and Trail, where the horse/human team have to surmount various obstacles and challenges in a set pattern, picking up different gaits on cue at precisely designated markers. All the classes were in the big ring except the trail course, which was constructed outside the ring.

Now, I knew my horse was no pleasure horse, and her conformation made collection difficult for her. But our relationship was wonderful, and she certainly would shine up brilliantly. I hadn't taken a lesson with Celia in a while, because I worked with her every day riding different horses, turning back for her, and she would bang on me just like she did when I took a lesson so I thought I was doing OK. But I asked her if she could give me a few pointers for the show. A lesson just before I go.

"Uh-unh," she said. "You're gonna need a lot of work. We need to start now."

The ring at Louise's farm was usually set up with obstacles, so she and her sister could keep tuned. Celia showed up and set up a course for me: Track right around that cone; pick up the lope at that rail; come around; break down to a trot, over the cross rail, right by the mounting block; walk when you get to me; pick up the trot at that fencepost; when you get to the mounting block again, pick up the lope, and lope three times around this half of the ring.

I couldn't do it. I missed my marks, stumbled over the cross rail, slid in to a walk, and started late. Chey fell in to the left, picked up the wrong lead, bowed out her ribs, and lurched into the canter leaning on her front end. Good grief.

"OK. What happened?" Where should I start? Half the time, I didn't even *know* what happened. Somewhere, deep down inside me, I wanted to cry. It didn't help that Louise and Victoria, who recognized Celia as someone worth listening to, had brought lawn chairs and an umbrella into the ring to watch! Right then, I wished they'd brought the margaritas, too, because I could use one.

Celia started banging. "Trot off," she'd say. I'd trot off. "Not like that! Don't come in here riding like a cowboy. Sit tall. Put your shoulders back so your shoulder blades are flat. Head up. Chin out. You're showing now. Be proud of your horse and yourself." I scrambled to comply. "Do a roll back." I did, looking at the ground where my horse would put her front foot. "You see money down there? Then keep your eyes up!" And on we went.

I think we managed to work together two more times before

the show. "Don't ride so hard; just let her float under you."
"Don't let her do that!" "Keep your eyes up." "Hold her ribs in,
hold, hold, hold, hold, hold!" "WRONG LEAD!" "Halt
straight." "Fix that!" "Don't let her get away with that!" We
were to have one more lesson before the show, but as it happened, we couldn't. The schedules just didn't mesh.

Day before the show, I had a pony party in the afternoon but
showed up early to prepack the truck and trailer to the extent I
could. Celia lent me her show halter and a saddle blanket with
pink trim, to match my pinstriped pink broadcloth shirt. My
show attire was going to be much more modest than anyone
else's. I didn't have a lot of bling and what I had, I didn't want to
wear at my first show. If I embarrassed myself, I didn't want to
do it in sequins and turquoise suede. I did the pony party, and
when I went to start the pony van going home, it wouldn't comply. Fortunately, it was only a modest delay—a phone call from
a staffer gave me the trick—but I didn't get home until about
9:00 p.m., then had to make dinner and my lunch for tomorrow
and set everything up at home, and wake up at 4:45 a.m. so I
could have a good breakfast, my requisite coffee, and be at the
barn by 6:15. I would be trailering with Jill, in her trailer. We
wanted to get there ahead of time, to walk the horses over the
grounds, and deal with any spooky issues regarding the loudspeakers, the signage, the generator, or whatever. That proved to
be prudent.

Celia had e-mailed me the night before the show. "Remember, you have a job to do, just like you did every day this year
for me on Zip. Go into your classes and communicate to the
horse what it is she has to do for you. Things won't be perfect.
Don't let it distract you. There is not a horse there who will be
error-free. Breathe, maintain your focus, think of your job, and
enjoy the day. I believe in you and Chey. Ride for me."

"I'm there!" I responded. "This is about Chey and me, doing what we do every day, trying to do it better each time. We're just going to be doing it in a different place. I know you'll be with us."

"That's exactly right," she replied. "I am always there with you."

So we got to the show. Leaving the horses in the trailer, we went to sign in, pay our fees, and get our numbers. Louise had told me all about this, and that I would have to look on the signs to find out my patterns for showmanship and trail. I got my number, I signed up for each class, or event, I was entered in, and then went back and we unloaded the horses. Chey was pretty up; she had never encountered loudspeakers before to my knowledge. Took a little getting used to, but I never felt she was about to leave me or might hurt me. Showmanship was first. I

Dressed up for Showmanship

put Celia's lucky halter with the big silver conchos on her, and down we went to the ring.

Most of these horses were quarter horses; many of them were registered and pedigreed. You could tell, whenever the prizes were announced, and the rider had two names and the horse had three. Chey has no pedigree. I don't know her breeding. I don't even know her age, although I guess she's about seventeen.

Chey and I had worked on Showmanship about three times before, but she was quiet and attentive. We did our patterns. I moved correctly when the judge circled us in her inspection, and we picked up the trot together and halted together. I turned around and tried to restrain the grin. I had no expectations. I was just loving the chance to show off my little horse.

There were about eight in this class. We were dismissed and headed out back to the trailers to tack up our horses and get ready for the next event. Another division filed in to start their classes.

Extended trot, Equitation

I saddled her up, pink pad and all, and mounted up. There was a little warm-up area out of sight of the show grounds, and we headed over there. She was a little nervous, but I just asked more of her, so her mind would stay with me rather than with her friends from the barn who were now out of sight. It was a little hard to get her quiet, get her to move in a slow, rhythmic way; but we got there, doing our thing, making our nice upright turns, quiet stops, soft backing up. Then I came back to the show grounds and heard on the loudspeakers the winners

We won?!

for Green Horse Showmanship. "First place: Blah-blah-blah on blah-blah-blah; second place: blah-blah-blah on blah-blah-blah; third place: blah-blah-blah on blah-blah-blah . . . fourth place, number 382, Stephanie Rogers and Cheyenne!" WOW! I won a ribbon! I rode down to the judge's stand to pick it up. I texted Celia: "First show; first class; first ribbon! Fourth!" "AWE-SOME!" she texted back. "Keep me apprised!"

My day was made. I couldn't believe it. I can't believe my

My belt of ribbons

head didn't split from the grin I couldn't suppress for the rest of the day. We had four more classes, and I just had a ball. Chey got better and better. She did her best against all the pedigreed horses, and I just loved her to pieces.

The show lasted from 8:00 a.m. to about 3:00 p.m. I ended the day with: Fifth Place in Road Hack, Fourth Place in Showmanship, Second Place in Equitation, First Place in Pleasure, First Place in Trail, and Reserve Champion for the Green Horse Division!

I entered five classes and came home with six ribbons!

After the show, a woman came up to me and asked if I would be interested in selling Chey to her. And I realized: No, I was not. I would sell my blood before I sold this horse.

———

The day after the show was the closing on the house. J and I met at the bank with our respective lawyers. I bought him out of his share of the property we bought together seventeen years and three cats ago. Owning a house together was not right for us. He was buying a house around the corner. He was storing his stuff here for a while; we agreed he would continue to pay the Dish bill while his stuff is here, so I could continue to watch the classic movies I love. He would be coming over later in the week to watch a game he couldn't get at home. I would probably give him back a set of keys. So I could ask him to watch the cats for me, if I decided to go away. And we would be going to his grandnephew's first birthday party next Sunday.

I have a horse, a house, a truck, and a horse trailer. I would never have believed it. I'm a believer, now. When you believe, the possibilities are endless. Believe.

Postscript: What I Learned from Chey

If the past does not serve you, let it go. Take the emotion out of it. If you want to communicate with someone, you need to do it on their terms, not yours. Pay attention. Think positive.

Let It Go

There is no need to hold on to anything, and I mean, anything, that does not provide you with positive feedback. Old hurts, injustices, and torts are past. There is nothing you can do about them now, except try to understand those events. This means thinking about things in a different light.

Chey certainly had reason to dismiss the entire human race, given her background. Misused, misunderstood, hurt; and still forced to live in a human world. Who could blame her for being suspicious and defensive when she came to me? Who would not envy the relationship I have with my horse now? It would not have been possible, if Chey held on to her past in favor of her present. If she had not been "present," she could not have been open to a different life in which she was treated fairly and recognized for her try.

Me, too. I approached my life defensively, just like Chey did, waiting for the next blow, the next disappointment. Being with her and helping her through her fears and anxieties showed me so much about my own. But it helps to look at things as I think horses do: Stuff doesn't happen *to you*, it just happens. Deal with it. If something bad happened in the past, it will take a lot of good to get past it, but you can get past it. You can replace it it with something positive, and the more good stuff you have, the more the bad stuff gets squeezed out. I also learned: *That which you pay attention to, you will have more of in your life.* The more time you spend going over the bad stuff, the larger its footprint in your life. Be like a horse. Learn your lesson and move on.

Take the Emotion Out of It

This is, of course, difficult, and is very much related to letting go. After a lifetime of running from painful emotions, they had become friends. They were dependable. No risk. I knew who to blame. Me. It was safe. It gives the illusion of control. It was just god-awful, but it must be possible for people to enjoy hurting themselves, because as I look at it now, I can say I must have, to cling to that hurt for so long. Let it go. And when I did, things got better between me and Chey. We began communicating better. Getter lighter, quicker movement with less and less, until now, it feels, when Chey and I are really in synch, that we are indeed dancing. And when Chey and I began communicating this way, something else happened to my human side. I began to communicate better in general.

In retrospect, I can see the difference between the way I used to communicate with my environment, and the way I do now. Like horses, I am a prey animal, or at least that's the way I've always felt. My reflex was to run, at the first suggestion of criticism, displeasure, disapproval. When I'd see horses spook at stuff that seems ordinary to us, like a bucket or a broom, I'd think they're nuts, but it made me think about how I reacted to the things I perceived as threats. Just like them, I wheeled and bolted first chance I got. But I'd work with Chey a little, with the ropes, with tarps, and I could see her realizing that some of this stuff was not a threat at all. I decided it would be better to be like Chey. Maybe I would find that not everything I thought was a threat, was. And that's exactly what I did find. She made me brave enough to find out.

Communicating on Their Terms

I am often reminded of the situation where you see someone, presumably American, perhaps in Italy, trying to communicate with an Italian in English. The Italian doesn't understand, so the American starts saying it louder. Eventually, the American is hollering at the Italian, who just shrugs his shoulders and walks away. The moral to that story is obvious. It becomes very clear with horses.

By understanding their priorities (food, position in the hierarchy, safety, avoiding work), their language (body position, eyes, energy), and their incentives (pressure and release), you communicate much more successfully. As you refine your skills of observation and physicality, you get even better.

And not only horses. People too respond better when their interests and desires are being served; and how much more willing are they to lean into it, when they are led by respect, versus fear or pain. While the stick has its place, the carrot is always preferable. Positive reinforcement is better for you and the universe.

Pay Attention

I experienced a lot of my life though my head. Thoughts, emotions, accusations, fear, anxiety swirled around in such a whirlpool it was all I could do to hold on. It was so consuming, I couldn't actually pay attention to what was going on. If you're stuck in your head, and not paying attention to the environment, you cannot respond appropriately to it. Once you've taken the emotion out of it, you can observe much more clearly. This will enable much better responses, and better outcomes.

Paying attention is a skill that horses possess to a highly refined degree. Striving for that level of awareness is a productive discipline for humans. The greater my awareness of my environment became (as opposed to my awareness of what was in my head), the more fully I began to participate in my life, and the richer and more satisfying it became.

Think Positive

After that grueling two first years with horses, I wound up with one dominating thought: *I'm afraid of falling off. I don't want to get hurt.* Every horse I rode, every horse I approached, there was that thought in my mind, *I'm afraid of falling off.* Many of the great horsemen maintain that riding is 90 percent mental. And the first rule not only for horses but for life is: *Think positive.*

Deepak Chopra has said that you need only to want a thing, and the universe reshapes so as to deliver it to you. Quantum physics says, that in a very real sense, the outcome of the experiment depends upon what the observer is looking for. So what you think, you are. Negative thinking has negative outcomes. My whole life was a demonstration of this. I thought so poorly about myself, and the universe accommodated me by creating that as my reality.

Sometimes, the only thing holding you back is what you believe. Chey has taken responsibility for my heart; she has given me the gift of believing that I will not fall off, I will not be hurt. I can do it. I can ride. I can handle it. Chey and Celia had to do a lot of work to get me there, but they didn't give up on me. So when I got on Dixie one day, there was a new companion in my head, a little voice that said, *You are staying on. You can ride this horse . . .*

And I did. I relaxed She relaxed. I felt her. We started communicating. I used my hands; she responded. I stayed in the saddle; we stayed *ensemble*. When I got off Dixie at the end of that lesson, I was a changed person. The change was in my mind, and it's stuck. Now, for all the daily crises of normal life, I have a new mantra: *I can ride this horse. I can do this.*

And Finally: The Cure for Loneliness

Part of what made life so miserable through the awful years of depression and self-accusation was loneliness. The sense that no one loved me, even though I had friends who did, who evidenced it in innumerable late-night phone calls where they would try to hold me back so I wouldn't go over the edge. Thank you, Jeff; thank you, Fred F., and thank you, Fred S., who's dead. But, of course, there was nothing they could say or do that could last longer than an echo, because their kindnesses fell into a bottomless pit. There was no "there" there. There was just the swirling whirlpool of disgust that dragged everything I did and everything I thought into its insatiable core. No earthly force could resist its gravity.

Until this horse. When this troubled animal began to trust and respect me, something changed—or opened—or began to slow. When this large creature, who could have ended my life in an instant, instead accepted me as her leader and gave me her service, she gave my life meaning and value. I often say that I feel my life began when I met Chey. Perhaps that is more than a metaphor. She believed in me. I began to believe in me.

So many friends have believed in me, and tried to convince me of my worth, but for some reason the human effort failed. More than twenty years of medication, therapy, and time spent in "the rooms" of twelve-step programs did not achieve as much as time spent with this horse. Perhaps it is because my friends were only people, but every time you get on a horse, you become more than human. Without words, but with the trust in her heart and the strength of her back, Chey showed me the way until I could find it myself.

The pride I took in our progress was richer than anything else I'd known, and lasted well beyond the echo. It stayed with me. It glowed in me every time I went to my horse and saw her sweet face, and her willing step into the halter. It was a foundation. We built on it, until I found, to my surprise, I had become someone who was . . . OK. And now, I find, I am no longer afraid of being alone. The jaws of the past no longer bite as they once did.

So, for me, the antidote to loneliness proved to be self-respect. Self-love is still a little ways off, but I know if I keep riding the horse in the direction she's going, I will find that, too.

Epilogue

After six more horse shows, Chey and I won the 2015 season championship. At the annual banquet on February 27, 2016, we were awarded a two-foot tall trophy with our names engraved on it, and I received a jacket proclaiming "2015 SDHPA Champion, Green Horse Division, Western," big as life.

Then, two weeks after we received our trophy, when this book was in the final stages of production, I got a call that Cheyenne was colicking. I raced to the barn to find her in the aisle, on the ground, writhing, with Louise and a boarder holding ropes to try to prevent her from rolling. The vet came, began treatment, and Chey seemed to be responding favorably. I decided to spend the night next to her in the barn. Around one thirty in the morning, I could see she was in distress again, stamping and looking at her flanks. When I called the equine hospital, they told me to get her there immediately. Louise jumped out of bed in the middle of a frigid night to hook up a horse trailer in total darkness, and we rushed her to the hospital.

Every effort was made to move the impaction that had begun to swell her colon. But every single effort failed. Chey was heading toward an intestinal rupture, which would have been both fatal and excruciating. I knew what I had to do.

Chey followed me like the good horse she was, loose line, at my shoulder, without hesitation or question, into the large padded room with the drain in the floor. Louise and another dear friend grabbed my upper arms just as my legs collapsed; and, with tears in her eyes, the veterinarian who had tried to save her pushed the plunger on the syringe. About twenty hours after I got the call, my beloved Chey died peacefully and without distress at 3:23 p.m. on March 13, 2016.

There never lived a horse more generous than Chey. There never lived a horse who was better loved. She was mourned by an entire community, and she will live in my heart forever.

Glossary

Alpha mare: A herd of horses is naturally hierarchical, and it is dominated by one mare, called the alpha mare. She is the one who leads the herd, decides when and where to eat or drink, when to rest and when to move. The stallion has two jobs, and they are to breed the mares and protect his privileges in that department. The alpha mare does the rest.

Arabian: A breed of horse, small, graceful, renowned for their beauty, intelligence, and stamina. They tend to be lively and excitable, or "hot."

Bay: A brown horse with black mane and tail is called a bay. There may also be white markings on the legs or the face.

Belgian: A breed of horse, a draft horse bred to pull, large, powerful, usually honey-colored with a pale mane and tail.

Bit: The metal part of a bridle that fits in the horse's mouth. There is a gap in the horse's teeth between the front incisors and the back molars that looks like it was designed to carry a bit. Bits come in more varieties than can be named, and each design when acted upon by the rider by using the rein(s), will put pressure on different parts of the horse's mouth and head, to communicate information and encourage certain responses. Bits that do not have a shank, like a simple snaffle, offer no leverage; i.e., if the rider pulls the rein with a pound of force, the horse will feel a pound of pressure. If the bit has a shank, an extension hanging off the lateral side of the bit, the force of the rider's pull can be multiplied many times. Certain bits encourage flexibility; others encourage straightness; some can encourage the horse to carry his head "on the vertical," meaning the bone in the front of a horse's face, from forelock to nose, is vertical. This is not merely a headset; a vertical headset on its own may be pretty, but what is really wanted is for the horse to be going in a collected frame (i.e., moving with impulsion, with the abdominals lifted and the back gently rounded). One outcome of a collected frame done properly is that the head will be "on the vertical."

Box stall: A stall in the shape of a box, ten square feet more or less. The horse is loose in the stall, can turn around, lie down, etc., versus a straight stall. *See also* straight stall, p. 271.

Bridle: Equipment usually made of leather that straps around a horse's head, enabling the rider to communicate with the horse by the use of reins and a bit.

Buck Brannaman: A gifted horseman and clinician, he follows in the footsteps of horsemen like Ray Hunt and Tom Dorrance, the modern fathers of humane horsemanship, who advocate using the natural instincts and language of horses as a means of gaining their cooperation.

"Bute": Phenylbutazone, an NSAID used to reduce inflammation and pain in non-humans.

Canter or lope: A three-beat gait, faster than a walk or a trot, slower than a gallop. Canter is the term used in English riding (defined on p. 265), lope the term used in western riding (defined on p. 272).

Cavaletti: A long pole, usually about eight to ten feet long and about four to five inches in diameter. It is a training tool. It can be laid flat on the ground, or lifted on blocks to make jumps of various heights. It encourages a horse to pick her feet up; it can be used as an aide to lengthen or shorten the horse's stride (important when doing jumps or obstacles); as an aide in teaching lead changes (*see* p. 268); and in many other ways.

Centered Riding: The name for the teaching of Sally Swift, a marvelous horsewoman who re-imagined equitation as a combination of physical and mental alignment. It borrows from Alexander Technique, which focuses on spinal alignment, and has as its fundamentals such concepts as "soft eyes," "breathing," and "centering," which is similar to the same concept as expressed in t'ai chi. Swift was diagnosed with scoliosis at age seven, which encouraged her to develop her theories. Her practice of what she preached enabled her to eventually abandon the back brace she had worn for years. There are now Centered Riding certification programs and schools all over the world.

Collection: It is a way in which the horse carries his body in which it is balanced and strong. It starts with impulsion; then there is a roundness to the horse in which the abdomen is lifted, the hindquarters are under the body, the neck is pleasantly rounded. This position causes the weight to be evenly distributed fore and aft. It can be considered a "compression" of the two ends of the horse toward the middle, impulsion "contained." Think Lipizanner stallions of Vienna versus racehorses in full stride. *See* drawing on pp. 264 and 265.

Crossties: At some barns, horses are tied in the aisle by means of crossties; there is a rope with a clip hanging down from each side of the aisle in the center of the barn. The clip fastens

Collection at the trot

onto the ring of the halter, one on each side of the horse's face, to suggest to the horse to remain where she is for grooming or saddling. The lines are usually attached to the ceiling or a high beam with something breakable, like baling twine. The reason for this is, if a horse panics and rears or bolts, it is much safer to have the lines break free, because then there is less chance of the horse getting hurt or hurting others.

Cutting: In this western sport, the horse separates a calf or cow from the herd and keeps the calf or cow from running back by keeping his body between the calf and the herd. It requires an extremely athletic horse, of a compact build.

Deep digital flexor tendon: One of the tendons in the posterior aspect of a horse's front leg that is responsible for flexing, or bending, the pastern joint (the last joint on the bottom before the hoof). When a horse lands on the front leg too hard, the tendon can become overstretched or torn. It is an injury seen in jumping, but other activities, or even fooling around in the pasture, can create it.

Dressage: Literally, "training." It refers to training a horse (and rider) to a higher level in which both can perform very refined and advanced movements. Think, ballet for horses. The Lipiz-zaner stallions of Vienna are an example of the most advanced degree of this training, but all horses benefit from its principles, which include balance, cadence, rhythm, and lightness.

English riding: One of the two predominant styles of riding in the United States uses a smaller saddle without a horn (that bump in the front of a cowboy type saddle) and some form of snaffle bit. It is the style usually used in jumping, dressage and also just riding for fun. Police horses are generally in English tack.

Equitation: The study and practice of riding horses.

Extension: Think racehorses in full stride. The body is elon-gated, not rounded, and hind and front legs are stretching out at or as close to their maximum reach as possible. *See* drawing below.

Farrier: A blacksmith who specializes in shoeing horses. Every farrier is a blacksmith, but not every blacksmith is a farrier.

Floating: Horses' teeth grow for most of their lives, as one might expect in a grazing animal, so once or twice a year, it is good to have the horse dentist or vet come to check your horse's

Extension at the trot

mouth. They make sure the horse has not ground any sharp points into her teeth, which could interfere with eating or with the bit, and if she does, the vet will grind the teeth down with either a hand file or a power tool to eliminate the "hooks" and keep the horse comfortable. This is called floating. It is painless, although difficult for a human to watch!

Free walk: In dressage, most movement occurs with a high degree of collection. The free walk is the portion of a dressage trial where the horse is released from his collected frame and allowed to swing along "freely."

Gelding: A castrated male horse. Male horses are typically castrated, unless intended for breeding, which makes life a lot easier for everyone, including the horse.

Grade: A horse without a pedigree—i.e., a horse not registered with any breed or color association, like the American Quarter Horse Association.

Halter: Called a head collar in other English-speaking countries, it is made of rope or leather, and fits around the horse's head to make her easier to catch and lead. The lead line will clip onto it, usually under the chin. It has no bit, which is preferable for tying, unless the horse is very well trained to tie; if a horse pulled back or spooked while tied up with reins leading to a bit, it could do serious damage to her mouth and tongue.

Haunches in: A maneuver in which the horse is going forward, but the hindquarters are curled in to the center of the ring such that, for example, if the horse is going around the ring to the left, the right hind leg steps into the spot left by the left front leg. The horse will leave a track in three lines. *See* drawing on facing page.

Into the bridle: The horse can't be balanced if it is leaning into the reins or pulling on them. Riding the horse "into the bridle" means getting the horse to a place of balance in which it en-

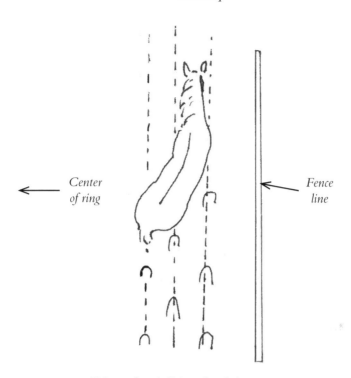

"Haunches in" is a flexibility exercise.

gages its hindquarters, providing impulsion, and is at the same time yielding to the reins. It is often associated with the idea of riding "from the back to the front." It is not achieved by pulling harder on the reins. That will accomplish just the opposite of the desired goal, and throw the horse onto his front end.

Inverting: When a horse has her head up and her back arched like a letter "c" with the open side facing up, it's called being inverted. It is the opposite of the way you'd like the body to be, which is rounded with the back up and the abdominals lifted, and the head and neck nicely rounded.

Lateral movement: Horses can move not only forward and backward, but side to side. Sideways movement is called lateral movement.

267

Lead line: A rope of varying lengths, usually six to ten feet long, with a clip on one end to fasten to a halter.

Leads: This term describes which of the hind feet the horse launches from (and, consequently, which of her front feet hits the ground last) in a canter or lope. A canter or lope is a three-beat gait. The horse launches off one hind leg; the other hind leg and diagonal front leg hit the ground simultaneously; then the last front leg hits the ground and the stride begins again. If the horse launches off her right hind leg, the left front leg will be the last to hit the ground. The horse is on her left lead. You want this if the horse is traveling a small circle to the left, so she won't trip. Sometimes, one may "counter-canter" the horse, i.e., make her go to the left while on the right lead. This is a test of the horse's balance and obedience.

Leg yield: The horse is moving forward and sideways at the same time, as if he were tracing the hypotenuse of a triangle.

Lope: *See* canter, p. 262.

Lunging: A handler has a horse on a long (ten- to thirty-foot) line (the lunge line) and moves the horse around in a circle with the handler in the middle. The objective may be to check the horse's soundness before asking him to carry a saddle and a rider; to settle the horse down if he is excited, before riding him; to exercise the horse if he is recovering from an injury or if other conditions prevent him from being ridden; and for various other purposes.

Nibble net: A fishnet like thing to put on hay so horses can't eat it as quickly. Like people, horses love to eat and, like people, they will do it all day if they can. This is a good adaptation in the wild, but not such a good one when they have free access to as much hay as they want, as they do at my barn.

Quarter horse: Sometimes called America's Horse, it is a breed of horse developed in the United States from Thoroughbred, Arabian, and native breeds descended from horses the conquistadors brought to the Americas. They are of medium height with muscular builds and good minds. They are known for bursts of tremendous speed, quick stops, and turns. It is said a Quarter Horse can turn on a dime and give you back seven cents' change. They can run a quarter of mile faster than almost any other living thing (a cheetah might beat them over a short haul, but not over distance). They were developed for working cattle but are used in almost every equine pursuit.

Ramp load: A horse trailer with a ramp that drops down to facilitate loading.

Reining: Reining is a discipline within western riding, in which superb control is demonstrated with, ironically, a rein so loose it sags to the horse's knees. Hallmarks of the discipline include sliding stops, where the horse will slide on her hind legs for as much as twenty feet (she needs special shoes for this); increases and decreases in speed with no visible cues; and spins, a turn on the hindquarters in which the horse plants one hind leg in the dirt and spins around it, at dizzying speed. The horse goes from whirling dervish to completely motionless in an instant. Needless to say, this takes an extremely athletic and balanced horse, and advanced training.

Reins: The long leather strap(s) attached to the bit, an aide for the rider in communicating with the horse. Reins are also made of rope, horsehair, and/or nylon.

Rollback: An advanced maneuver in which the horse is going in one direction, halts in a collected manner (i.e., his hindquarters are underneath him), does a 180-degree turn lifting the front feet off the ground, and resumes travel in the opposite direction. It should be a smooth, uninterrupted motion. Very nice to look at, if done properly.

Round pen: As the name suggests, it is a round corral, usually six feet high or higher, fifty to sixty feet in diameter, used as a training tool. Because there are no corners for a horse to "hide" in, and it is a relatively controlled space, the round pen is useful in establishing the relationship you want with the horse (that is, the dominant role); and it is helpful for lots of things, like de-sensitizing horses to things they may encounter (ropes, feed bags, etc.); and working on "firsts," like first saddling, first bri-dling, first mounting. etc.

Saddle, saddle pad: The leather or synthetic equipment that goes on the horse's back from which the stirrups hang. A pad is typically put under the saddle to provide additional cushion for the horse and to keep the underside of the saddle clean.

Shoulder in: Similarly to "haunches in," the horse curls the forehand into the center, so that she leaves three tracks in the ground with the inside hind leg stepping into the spot the out-side front leg has just left. *See also* haunches in, p. 266.

Side pass: The horse moves sideways, with neither the head nor the tail leading. If done against a straight fence, the horse's body should be perfectly perpendicular, although a slight bend away from the direction of movement is acceptable (i.e., if the horse is moving left, his body may be curved slightly to the right).

Slant-load trailer: A trailer in which the horses instead of standing straight forward stand at an angle, e.g., left front to right rear, with dividers between them. Some consider it easier to balance in a moving vehicle in this position.

Standing wraps: A padded, pillowy square or rectangular cloth that is wrapped around the horse's leg(s) and secured with vet wrap (an Ace bandage for horses). It provides some support and protection for lower leg injuries.

Step-up trailer: A trailer in which the floor is raised a foot or more off the ground and the horse "steps up" to get into it.

Stirrup: A metal, wooden or plastic frame into which the rider puts his or her foot when riding a horse.

Stock trailer: A trailer with rails around the top of the perimeter, more open than other types, often with no dividers inside.

Stocked up: When a horse's activity is limited, sometimes fluid will collect in her lower legs, swelling them. This is called being stocked up. Usually, as soon as the horse can move around again, the condition resolves.

Straight stall: A stall in the shape of a rectangle in which the horse stands, sometimes tied. There is usually not enough room for horses to turn around in and it may be difficult for them to lie down or get up again if they do. Since horses generally sleep on their feet, this is not quite the hardship it might seem, although not being able to move around much is not great.

Tack: The generic term for the equipment one puts on a horse before riding: saddle and bridle generally, but can include martingales (designed to limit upward movement of the horse's head, come in several varieties); tie-downs (same thing, western style); breast collars (strap around the horse's chest to keep the saddle from slipping back); crupper (strap under the tail to keep saddle from slipping forward), etc.

Turn-back rider: In the sport of cutting, all the cutting horses do is cut. The cows are moved and managed by other mounted people. The "turn-back" riders guide the cow being worked to put the cow back into position so the cutting horse can work the cow until the human can "legally" quit the cow. There are rules about when that can happen, too.

Turn on the forehand, turn on the hindquarters: In a turn on the forehand, the horse's front legs remains in place and he makes a turn by moving his hindquarters around his front legs.

Ideally, the horse plants the inside front foot and swivels around it. A turn on the hindquarters is when the hind end is stationary and the front end moves around. Similarly, the horse should plant the inside hind foot and swivel around it.

Warmblood: A general term for a horse who is not "hot" (like an Arabian, which tends to be "up" and excitable) or "cold" (draft horses like Percherons and Clydesdales, which tend to be quieter and more level-headed), but in the middle. Warmbloods tend to be larger horses with good bone and muscle. They are favored in the sport of dressage.

Western movement: A term of art, the sort of movement you might expect to see in a good western style horse, i.e., low, level, smooth, swinging along.

Western riding: The other predominant style of riding in the United States. It uses a saddle with a horn, like you see American cowboys using.

Working walk: A basic working gait in which the horse is not just moseying along, but moving forward in a relaxed manner with energy and impulsion.

Acknowledgments

This book came in to being as the result of one institution and one individual. The institution is the Pawling Free Library, and the workshops, programs, special events, and general participation in the literary and salutary advancement of this lovely town in the Hudson Valley that gave me the venue in which to explore my story. The individual who had most to do with bringing this story to light is the most excellent Dr. Robin Lester, author, historian and mentor. His memoir writing workshop at the Pawling Free Library provided three things a writer needs: an opportunity, an audience, and a periodic deadline. Not only did he provide me the structure I needed to pursue this undertaking: His kindness, encouragement, and always constructive support have done more than I can say to keep me enthused and on the right track. Thank you, Robin. Awfully glad I met you.

Finally, my thanks would not be complete without recognizing my wonderful editor, Joan Giurdanella, who made everything she touched better. Thank you, Joan!

About the Author

Stephanie Rogers is a New York City native, born in Queens and living in Manhattan until relocating to Dutchess County in the mid "oughties" (2006). She spent fifteen years in the theater, during which time she was a mezzo-soprano with the Light Opera of Manhattan; a voice-over talent; a dancer with Morelli Jazz; and a member of the More than Mime Theater Project. When it looked like theater would not pay the bills, she switched to film, working primarily as an assistant director on a number of low-budget to no-budget movies. The necessity of earning a living prompted her to return to school, and she attended Baruch College of the City University of New York at night while working full-time during the day at an international financial institution. She graduated with a bachelor of science degree in finance. Eighteen years on Wall Street enabled her to retire early to pursue a lifetime dream of having a horse, and writing. She and her horse now compete and have a substantial number of Champion and Reserve Champion ribbons to their credit, including the SDHPA 2015 Grand Championship for their division. She is currently on the Board of Directors of Pawling Public Radio, and is a writer and producer for the station that streams 24/7 at Pawlingpublicradio.org, and broadcasts locally at 103.7 on the FM dial. This is her first book. She is currently working on a second book, a murder mystery, which will draw upon her Wall Street experiences. None of which included actual, you know, murder.

Her website is *Horsetalker.com*.

Made in the USA
Columbia, SC
10 May 2018